Patc

200 Q&A

1st ed.

WITHDRAWN

Patchwork
200 Q&A

Questions answered on everything from basic blocks
to accurate binding

Jake Finch

Chief Contributor
Victoria L. Tymczyszyn

BARRON'S

A Quantum Book

Copyright © 2011 Quantum Publishing

First edition for North America and the Philippines published in 2011 by
Barron's Educational Series, Inc.

All inquiries should be addressed to:
Barron's Educational Series, Inc.
250 Wireless Boulevard
Hauppauge, New York 11788
www.barronseduc.com

ISBN-13: 978-0-7641-6374-6

Library of Congress Control Number: 2010940193

This book is published and produced by
Quantum Books
6 Blundell Street
London N7 9BH

QUMQ2QA

Project Editor: Samantha Warrington
Production: Rohana Yusof
Photographer: Marcos Bevilacqua
Design: Norma Martin
Publisher: Sarah Bloxham

Printed in China by Midas Printing International Ltd.

9 8 7 6 5 4 3 2 1

CONTENTS

Introduction   6

How To Use This Book   7

Chapter 1:   About Patchwork   8

Chapter 2:   Four-Patch Blocks   14

Chapter 3:   Nine-Patch Blocks   26

Chapter 4:   Sixteen-Patch Blocks   50

Chapter 5:   Thirty-Six and Sixty-Four Patch Blocks   66

Chapter 6:   No-Grid Blocks and Quilts   84

Chapter 7:   Patchwork Basics   110

Chapter 8:   Designing Patchwork and Using Color   120

Chapter 9:   Choosing and Cutting Fabric   134

Chapter 10:   Machine Piecing   146

Chapter 11:   Basic Block Construction   160

Chapter 12:   Rows and Borders   172

Chapter 13:   Putting It All Together   180

Chapter 14:   Binding and Finishing   202

Templates   214

Index   224

INTRODUCTION

Twenty years ago, I made my first quilt. It was almost an accident, the result of a moment's inspiration after seeing a pattern in *Better Homes & Garden* magazine. The product of this burst of sewing effort was too bulky, from the result of the denim/calico combo of fabrics that I selected; too heavy, from the large plastic buttons used to tie the quilt into bondage; and too big, because I'd ambitiously constructed a king-sized monstrosity that was destined to cover our circa-1980's water bed. I loved the darned thing! To this day I resurrect The Beast, as I dubbed my first quilt, and often bring it to quilt guilds and beginners' classes that I teach to assure those newbie stitchers that we all must start somewhere.

Since sewing those first pieces on my machine, I have created a career based on cutting up perfectly good yards of fabric and sewing them together into perfectly better quilt blocks, then to be sewn into quilts. My quilts are used as bedcoverings, clothing, home decor items, bags, purses, book covers, and so much more. The basic principles of quilt making can be applied to so many other creative endeavors that one can spend a lifetime without ever tiring of switching on the sewing machine.

Join me and my wonderful friend, Vicki Tymczyszyn, as we show you how you too can insanely slice your fabrics only to sew them together again into beautiful patchwork quilts.

HOW TO USE THIS BOOK

Patchwork is the art of sewing together pieces of fabric to create new patterns. The secret to creating perfect patterns lies in the accurate cutting of those fabric pieces; these "patches" are sewn together to form the blocks that make up patchwork design.

This book, therefore, begins with diagrams of some of the most popular patchwork blocks. You will also find charts that indicate what size you need to cut your patches to achieve different sized finished blocks.

Chapters 2 to 7 cover the different block options; in Chapters 8 to 13 you will find all you need to know about putting patchwork together. You'll learn about essential equipment; how to design a patchwork quilt and how to work with color; information on choosing and using fabrics; and how to piece together your patches and blocks.

In Chapters 14 and 15 you'll find out how to turn your finished patchwork into a quilt and how to finish off everything neatly – and creatively. And any templates that you'll need are at the very end of this book.

1　What is a quilt?

2　What is patchwork?

3　What are some examples
　　of traditional patchwork?

4　How can patchwork be used
　　in contemporary quilts?

1

ABOUT PATCHWORK

Question 1:
What is a quilt?

A quilt is a textile created from three layers: a top, often made from patches of fabrics, a soft middle layer called batting, and a backing piece of fabric. The three layers are sewn together, either by hand or machine, and this sewing is called the quilting. The word "quilt" can be a noun, as in "the quilt," or a verb, as in "to quilt." Quilts are commonly thought of as bed coverings, but some quilts are designed to be art, and are found hanging in museums and galleries, and still more quilts are made into serviceable items like placemats and clothing.

A quilt can be made from simple shapes and construction techniques, or can be made using complicated techniques at an expert level.

BELOW A classic sampler quilt; this example features many different patchwork blocks set in a medallion style with a central focus.

Question 2:
What is patchwork?

There are several different techniques used to create quilt tops, and patchwork is the most common. Patchwork refers to pieces of fabric that are cut up and reassembled into a pattern before being sewn together by hand or machine. Generally, these pieces are made into blocks, and the blocks make up the design of the quilt top. Patchwork quilts can be made with one or several blocks repeating to create the design, or with each block different.

Most patchwork blocks have geometric designs, incorporating squares, triangles, and rectangles, but curves, circles, and more obscure geometric shapes can also be used. While patchwork blocks are often symmetrical, there is no set rule for this, and there are many traditional patchwork blocks made from asymmetrical patterns.

Throughout the ages, quilters have stretched or broken the rules to create new techniques and styles within the quilt genre, and patchwork is no exception. What you'll find in these pages is a good overall look at popular patchwork blocks, how to construct them, and illustrations of finished samples. There are also projects to inspire you. From this introduction, you might choose to develop your own style and design aesthetic with which to create patchwork quilts. Always remember that quilt making is supposed to be fun, and that for every technique there will be alternative ways to do the same thing. Always find what works best for you.

Question 3:
What are some examples of traditional patchwork?

The following are just SOME of the many variations by which quilters use patchwork in their quilts.

ABOVE AND LEFT Traditional quilt examples. Clockwise from top left: medallion with an appliqué center; lonestar; and friendship quilts.

Question 4:
How can patchwork be used in contemporary quilts?

There's no rule that says patchwork can only be used in traditional quilts. Many contemporary quilters embrace patchwork blocks and incorporate them into quilt designs that clearly say, "TODAY!" This might be achieved through color/fabric choices or through the overall design. Some quilters will alter blocks to make them look fresh and create interest.

Here are a few examples of contemporary quilts using patchwork blocks:

ABOVE Another trick that turns a traditional quilt design into something more contemporary is to have the top's blocks "bleed" into the borders.

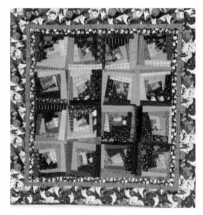

ABOVE Skewed blocks quilt: This quilt shows how a traditional Log Cabin block can be given an updated look just by turning it off-center.

ABOVE Modern color choice: Color and texture are probably the best tools a quilter has for designing.

5 What is a Four-Patch block?

6 What is a Flying Geese block?

7 What is a Pinwheel block?

8 What is a Windmill block?

9 What is a Dutchman's Puzzle block?

10 What is a Broken Dishes block?

11 What is a Bow Tie block?

12 What is a Spools block?

13 What is an Old Maid's Puzzle block?

14 What is an Orange Peel block?

15 What is a Capital T block?

2 FOUR-PATCH BLOCKS

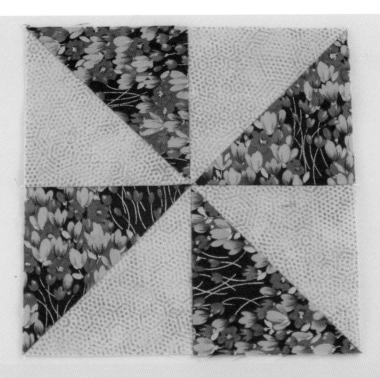

Question 5:
What is a Four-Patch block?

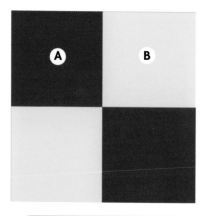

A simple Four-Patch block has two pairs of contrasting fabrics, arranged like a checkerboard. Each square can be made from one fabric, or from a smaller, pieced design made into a square. Many traditional blocks are created from variations of the Four-Patch block.

The Four-Patch block's construction is the same whether the individual units are squares or something more complicated. Once the four units are sewn, sew the top two squares together for the first row, the bottom two squares together for the second row. To finish, sew the two rows together.

HOW IT'S DONE

1 Cut the patches as shown based on the desired finished block size.

2 Follow directions for Four-Patch blocks as provided in Question 145 in Chapter 11.

PATCH	No	3"	6"	9"	12"	15"
A	2	2"	3 ½"	5"	6 ½"	8"
B	2	2"	3 ½"	5"	6 ½"	8"

Question 6:
What is a Flying Geese block?

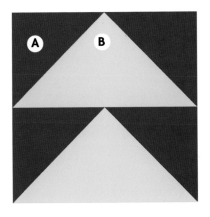

HOW IT'S DONE

1 Cut the patches as shown based on the desired finished block size.

2 Follow directions for Flying Geese Blocks as provided in Question 146 in Chapter 11.

3 Sew another Geese set.

4 Sew two Geese with right sides together and point of one unit aligned with bottom of other unit.

5 Press toward the top geese unit.

The name of the block comes from the "V" shaped flying formation geese use during their annual migrations. The large triangles, or "Vs", are the interpretation of the flying geese.

PATCH	No	6"	9"	12"	15"
A	4	3 ½"	5"	6 ½"	8"
B	2	3 ½" X 6 ½"	5" X 9 ½"	6 ½" X 12 ½"	8" X 15 ½"

Question 7:

What is a Pinwheel block?

A Pinwheel block looks like a child's pinwheel spinning in the wind. It's made from four identical half-square triangle units. The darker triangles face the same direction and appear to spin around the center.

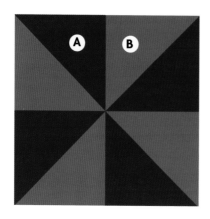

HOW IT'S DONE

1 Cut the patches as shown based on the desired finished block size.

2 Follow directions for making Half-Square triangles as provided in Question 147 in Chapter 11. Make two sets of Half-Square triangles.

3 Arrange patches according to diagram on left.

4 Follow directions for Four-Patch blocks as provided in Question 145 in Chapter 11.

PATCH	No	6"	9"	12"	15"
A	2	3 ⁷⁄₈"	5 ³⁄₈"	6 ⁷⁄₈"	8 ³⁄₈"
B	2	3 ⁷⁄₈"	5 ³⁄₈"	6 ⁷⁄₈"	8 ³⁄₈"

Question 8:

What is a Windmill block?

The Windmill block is a variation of the Pinwheel block. Slightly more sophisticated than the Pinwheel block, it uses the same design principle of triangles spinning around the center, one large and one small. In this case, each patch is made up of a Half-Square triangle and a Quarter-Square triangle.

PATCH	No	6"	9"	12"	15"
A	1	4 ¹⁄₄"	5 ³⁄₄"	7 ¹⁄₄"	8 ³⁄₄"
B	1	4 ¹⁄₄"	5 ³⁄₄"	7 ¹⁄₄"	8 ³⁄₄"
C	2	3 ⁷⁄₈"	5 ³⁄₈"	6 ⁷⁄₈"	8 ³⁄₈"

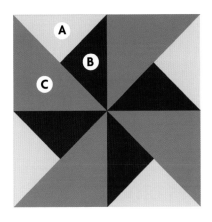

HOW IT'S DONE

1 Decide on the block's finished size from the chart.

2 Follow directions for Quarter-Square Triangles as provided in Question 149 in Chapter 11. Make two sets of Quarter-Square Triangles.

3 Arrange four patches according to diagram above.

4 Follow directions for Four-Patch blocks as provided in Question 145 in Chapter 11.

Question 9:

What is a Dutchman's Puzzle block?

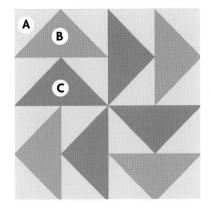

HOW IT'S DONE

1 Cut the patches as shown based on the desired finished block size.

2 Follow directions for Flying Geese Blocks as provided in Question 146 in Chapter 11. Make four AB units and four AC units.

3 Follow directions for Four-Patch blocks as provided in Question 145 in Chapter 11.

The Dutchman's Puzzle block uses Flying Geese blocks to create a pinwheel effect. It requires four Flying Geese blocks, positioned to look as if they are spinning around the center. Changing the fabrics for the 4 smaller center triangles can create a secondary design. The block shown here is in its simplest form.

PATCH	No	6"	9"	12"	15"
A	16	3 ½"	5"	6 ½"	8"
B	4	3 ½" X 6 ½"	5" X 9 ½"	6 ½" X 12 ½"	8" X 15 ½"
C	4	3 ½" X 6 ½"	5" X 9 ½"	6 ½" X 12 ½"	8" X 15 ½"

Question 10:

What is a Broken Dishes block?

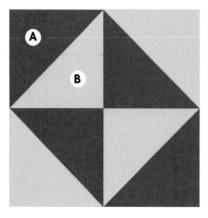

The Broken Dishes block is a Four-Patch block using several smaller triangles arranged in what might look like a random pattern to represent broken dishes that have been put back together.

HOW IT'S DONE

1 Cut the patches as shown based on the desired finished block size.

2 Follow directions for making Half-Square triangles as provided in Question 147 in Chapter 11. Make two sets of Half-Square triangles.

3 Arrange patches according to diagram above.

4 Follow directions for Four-Patch blocks as provided in Question 145 in Chapter 11.

PATCH	No	6"	9"	12"	15"
A	2	3 ⅞"	5 ⅜"	6 ⅞"	8 ⅜"
B	2	3 ⅞"	5 ⅜"	6 ⅞"	8 ⅜"

Question 11:

What is a Bow Tie block?

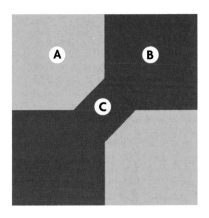

The Bow Tie block is a Four-Patch block using squares and triangles to look like a bow tie. When the block is set on-point, the bow tie is straight.

PATCH	No	3"	6"	9"	12"	15"
A	2	2"	3 ½"	5"	6 ½"	8"
B	2	2"	3 ½"	5"	6 ½"	8"
C	2	1"	2"	2 ¼"	3 ½"	4 ¼"

Question 12:
What is a Spools block?

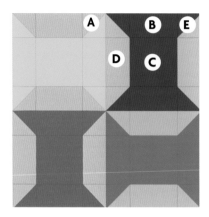

This block looks like four spools of thread on their sides. They are arranged in a Four-Patch format, making it easy to piece each spool. The spools themselves are Nine-Patch blocks.

HOW IT'S DONE

1 Cut the patches as shown based on the desired finished block size.

2 Follow directions for making Half-Square triangles as provided in Question 147 in Chapter 11. Make 8 sets total (two sets of each color) of Half-Square triangles. You'll have 16 Half-Square triangles (4 of each color) when done.

3 Assemble each colored spool's patches as follows:
- Row 1: AE, B, AE
- Row 2: D, C, D
- Row 3: AE, B, AE

When done, you'll have (4) AE spools, each of a different color.

4 Arrange spool units in Four-Patch block as shown. Follow directions for Four-Patch blocks as provided in Question 145 in Chapter 11.

PATCH	No	6"	9"	12"	15"
A	2 *	1 ⁵/₈"	2"	2 ³/₈"	2 ³/₄"
B	2 *	1 ¹/₄" X 2"	1 ⁵/₈" X 2 ¹/₄"	2" X 3 ¹/₂"	2 ³/₈" X 4 ¹/₄"
C	1 **	2"	2 ³/₄"	3 ¹/₂"	4 ¹/₄"
D	8	1 ³/₄" X 2"	1 ⁵/₈" X 2 ³/₄"	2" X 3 ¹/₂"	2 ³/₈" X 4 ¹/₄"
E	8	1 ⁵/₈"	2"	2 ³/₈"	2 ³/₄"

*2 ea. color, 4 colors total **1 ea. color, 4 colors total

Question 13:

What is an Old Maid's Puzzle block?

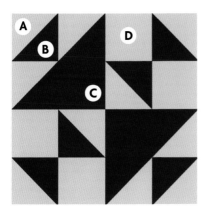

This is somewhat more complicated to construct because the corners must be made before the block is assembled. Take each step in turn, and you'll have fewer problems.

HOW IT'S DONE

1 Cut the patches as shown, based on the desired finished block size.

2 Using A and B squares, follow directions for making Half-Square triangles as provided in Question 147 in Chapter 11. Make (3) sets of Half-Square triangles.

3 With remaining (2) A squares, draw line diagonally through middle and cut in half. Sew A triangles to each B side of AB Half-Square triangle units. Press seams to A triangles.

4 On C patch, draw line diagonally through middle and cut in half. Sew C triangle to A/AB/A unit per diagram. Press seam to C triangle. Repeat once more.

5 Assemble alternate corners as follows:
• Row 1: D, AB unit
• Row 2: AB unit, D
Repeat once more.

6 Arrange units in Four-Patch blocks as shown. Follow directions for Four-Patch blocks as provided in Question 145 in Chapter 11.

PATCH	No	6"	9"	12"	15"	
A	5	4 1/4"	5 3/4"	7 1/4"	8 3/4"	
B	3	4 1/4"	5 3/4"	7 1/4"	8 3/4"	
C	1	3 7/8"	5 3/8"	6 7/8"	8 3/8"	
D	4	2"	2 3/4"	3 1/2"	4 1/4"	

Question 14:
What is an Orange Peel block?

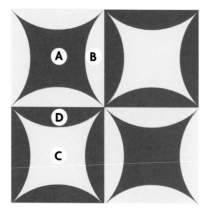

Some quilters prefer to appliqué this Four-Patch block's curved pieces, but with a little practice, curved piecing is easy to achieve. (Instructions for curved piecing are found on page 157.) If you choose to piece it, refer to the templates in the back of the book.

(Instructions for curved piecing are found on page 157.)

HOW IT'S DONE

1 Cut the patches and template pieces as shown based on the desired finished block size.

2 Sew B to A matching centers and ends for all four sides. Press each side outward. Repeat to make 2 patches.

3 Sew D to C matching centers and ends for all four sides. Press each side outward. Repeat to make 2 patches.

4 Arrange units in Four-Patch block as shown. Follow directions for Four-Patch blocks as provided in Question 145 in Chapter 11.

PATCH	No	6"	9"	12"	15" *
A	2	4" X 4"	5" X 5"	7" X 7"	8" X 8"
B	8	2" X 4"	2 1/2" X 5"	3" X 7"	3 1/2" X 8"
C	2	4" X 4"	5" X 5"	7" X 7"	8" X 8"
D	8	2" X 4"	2 1/2" X 5"	3" X 7"	3 1/2" X 8"

*all shapes are templates

This chart is for Question 15.

PATCH	No	6"	9"	12"	15"
A	4	2 7/8"	3 7/8"	4 7/8"	6 1/8"
B	1*	2 7/8"	3 7/8"	4 7/8"	6 1/8"
C	5**	1 7/8"	2 3/8"	2 7/8"	3 1/16"
D	20	1 7/8"	2 3/8"	2 7/8"	3 1/16"

*1 ea. color, 4 total **5 ea. color, 20 total

Question 15:
What is a Capital T block?

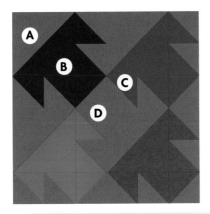

This is a tessellating block, where one T unit fits into another T unit turned in the opposite direction. It's an optical illusion and can be very effective visually. The T traditionally stood for "temperance," making this a popular block in the 1920s and 1930s when Prohibition was in force throughout the United States. The entire block is made from Half-Square triangles, large and small.

HOW IT'S DONE

1 Cut the patches as shown above based on the desired finished block size.

2 For the larger Half-Square triangles, use A and B squares and follow directions for making Half-Square triangles as provided in Question 147 in Chapter 11. Make (4) sets of Half-Square triangles. You'll have (8) Half-Square AB units when done, but you only need 4, one of each color, for one block. Save the remaining units for a second block.

3 Use C and D square for the smaller Half-Square triangles and repeat Half-Square Triangle directions. Make 20 sets of CD Half-Squares. You'll have (40) CD units when done, but you only need 20, 5 of each color, for one block. Save the remaining units for a second block.

4 Sew together 2 pairs of CD units for each color. You'll have 1 CD unit left by itself.

5 Assemble each "T" as follows, using the illustration above to place the units:
- Row 1: AB, CD pair
- Row 2: CD pair, CD

6 Sew the "T's" rows together. Repeat for other 3 colors.

7 Arrange T blocks in Four-Patch block as shown. Follow directions for Four-Patch blocks as provided in Question 145 in Chapter 11.

16 What is a Nine-Patch block?

17 What is a Double Nine-Patch block?

18 What is an Ohio Star block?

19 What is a Bear Paw block?

20 What is a Rail Fence block?

21 What is a Shoofly block?

22 What is a Churn Dash block?

23 What is a Friendship Star block?

24 What is a Birds in the Air block?

25 What is a Northwinds block?

26 What is a Twin Star block?

27 What is a Garden Square block?

28 What is a Dove in the Window block?

29 What is a Maple Leaf block?

30 What is a Fifty-Four Forty or Fight block?

31 What is a Road to Paradise block?

32 What is a Card Trick block?

33 What is a Variable Star block?

34 What is a Cat's Cradle block?

NINE-PATCH BLOCKS

Question 16:
What is a Nine-Patch block?

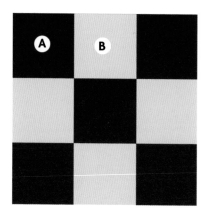

HOW IT'S DONE

1 Cut the patches as shown based on the desired finished block size.

2 Arrange the patches as shown. Sew rows as follows:

- Row 1: ABA
- Row 2: BAB
- Row 3: ABA

3 Sew Row 2 to Row 1.

4 Sew Row 3 to Row 2.

5 Press seams toward block's outside edge.

Similar to the Four-Patch blocks in its simplest form, the Nine-Patch block has one more row of squares across and one more row of squares down. Mastering this simple block will lead to many other block options because so many other blocks start with a Nine-Patch arrangement.

PATCH	No	3"	6"	9"	12"	15"	
A	5	1½"	2½"	3½"	4½"	5½"	
B	4	1½"	2½"	3½"	4½"	5½"	

Question 17:
What is a Double Nine-Patch block?

This Nine-Patch block is made up of simple Nine-Patch units. When used across an entire quilt, the effect is one of a simple chain moving diagonally across the quilt top. This makes it a perfect alternating block for a sampler quilt or a two-block quilt.

This block may be made in an alternating fashion with strip-piecing. If an entire quilt is to be made of this block as a chain quilt or in use as an alternating block, the strip-piecing method is recommended and will be described in a later chapter. The method described below is for one block only. This block can make use of

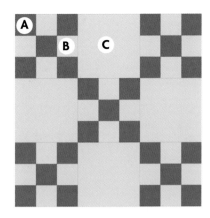

many fabric scraps and is charming when made in a variety of colors.

HOW IT'S DONE

1 Cut the patches as shown based on the desired finished block size.

2 Arrange squares as shown in smaller Nine-Patch units.

3 Sew two rows in A, B, A format. Sew one row in B, A, B format.

4 Press all seams toward darker fabric.

5 Sew alternating rows together to finish block. Press seams toward center row.

6 Repeat steps 2 to 5 (4) times to create (5) smaller Nine-Patch units

7 Arrange smaller Nine-Patch units with C squares as shown to create larger Nine-Patch block.

8 Arrange the patches as shown above. Sew rows as follows:

• Row 1: Nine-Patch, C, Nine-Patch
• Row 2: C, Nine-Patch, C
• Row 3: Nine-Patch, C, Nine-Patch

9 Sew Row 2 to Row 1.

10 Sew Row 3 to Row 2.

11 Press seams toward block's outside edge.

PATCH	No	9"	12"	15"	18"
A	25	1 1/2"	1 15/16"	2 3/16"	2 1/2"
B	20	1 1/2"	1 15/16"	2 3/16"	2 1/2"
C	4	3 1/2"	4 1/2"	5 1/2"	6 1/2"

Question 18:
What is an Ohio Star block?

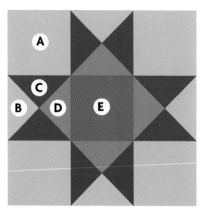

This Nine-Patch block uses Quarter-Square triangles as the star's points. This block is typical of the star blocks that were made throughout the state of Ohio during the 19th and 20th centuries, and are still popular there today.

PATCH	No	6"	9"	12"	15"
A	4	2 1/2"	3 1/2"	4 1/2"	5 1/2"
B	1	3 1/4"	4 1/4"	5 1/4"	6 1/4"
C	2	3 1/4"	4 1/4"	5 1/4"	6 1/4"
D	1	3 1/4"	4 1/4"	5 1/4"	6 1/4"
E	1	2 1/2"	3 1/2"	4 1/2"	5 1/2"

HOW IT'S DONE

1 Cut the patches as shown above based on the desired finished block size.

2 Cut each B, C and D patch diagonally from corner to corner twice, as in an X pattern. You will now have 4 triangles from B and D and 8 triangles from C.

3 Sew B triangles to C triangles following illustration for placement. Sew D triangles to C triangles as per illustration. Press seams toward C triangle in both sets of units. Sew BC unit to CD unit.

Press seam to one side. You should have (4) BCCD units.

4 Arrange the patches as shown above. Sew rows as follows:

- Row 1: A, BCCD, A
- Row 2: BCCD, E, BCCD
- Row 3: A, BCCD, A

5 Sew Row 2 to Row 1.

6 Sew Row 3 to Row 2.

7 Press seams toward block's outside edge.

Question 19:
What is a Bear Paw block?

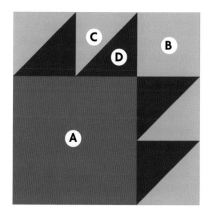

This block looks like the footprint a bear leaves when walking through the woods. The smaller triangles represent the bear's toes. Usually this block uses a different fabric for the pad of the paw and the toes, but it's your choice.

HOW IT'S DONE

1 Cut the patches as shown above based on the desired finished block size.

2 From C and D squares, follow directions for Half-Square triangles as provided in Question 147 in Chapter 11. Make two sets.

3 Sew two CD units together as shown and repeat once.

4 Sew B patch to top CD unit as shown. Press seam to B.

5 Sew A patch to bottom CD unit as shown. Press seam to A.

6 Sew top row (CD, B) to bottom row (A, CD). Press.

PATCH	No	6"	9"	12"	15"
A	1	4 1/2"	6 1/2"	8 1/2"	10 1/2"
B	1	2 1/2"	3 1/2"	4 1/2"	5 1/2"
C	2	2 7/8"	3 7/8"	4 7/8"	5 7/8"
D	2	2 7/8"	3 7/8"	4 7/8"	5 7/8"

Question 20:
What is a Rail Fence block?

This block is a good beginner's block because there are no bias edges to manipulate. It's made from three equal strips of fabric sewn together in rows, and it resembles the rows of a fence from the Old West. The top and bottom rows represent wooden fence rails and the center fabric represents the sky between them.

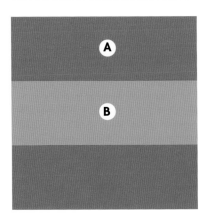

HOW IT'S DONE

1 Cut the patches as shown based on the desired finished block size.

2 Sew A strip to B strip, aligning the top and bottom of the strips. Pin if necessary.

3 Sew second A strip to other side of B strip.

4 Press seams toward center strip.

PATCH	No	6"	9"	12"	15"
A	2	2 ½" X 6 ½"	3 ½" X 9 ½"	4 ½" X 12 ½"	5 ½" X 15 ½"
B	1	2 ½" X 6 ½"	3 ½" X 9 ½"	4 ½" X 12 ½"	5 ½" X 15 ½"

Question 21:
What is a Shoofly block?

This is one of the simplest Nine-Patch blocks and is often used as a teaching tool for beginners since the components are only squares and half-square triangle units.

HOW IT'S DONE

1 Cut the patches as shown based on the desired finished block size.

2 With A and B squares, follow directions for Half-Square triangles as provided in Question 147 in Chapter 11. Make two sets.

3 Arrange the patches as shown above. Sew rows as follows:
- Row 1: AB, C, AB
- Row 2: C, D, C
- Row 3: AB, C, AB

4 Sew Row 2 to Row 1. Sew Row 3 to Row 2. Press seams to block's outside edge.

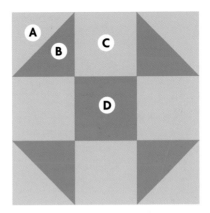

PATCH	No	6"	9"	12"	15"	
A	2	2 7/8"	3 7/8"	4 7/8"	5 7/8"	■
B	2	2 7/8"	3 7/8"	4 7/8"	5 7/8"	■
C	4	2 1/2"	3 1/2"	4 1/2"	5 1/2"	■
D	1	2 1/2"	3 1/2"	4 1/2"	5 1/2"	■

Question 22:
What is a Churn Dash block?

This block gets its name from the shape of the paddle used to churn butter. When the center square is a darker color, or even blue, this block is sometimes called Hole in the Barn Door.

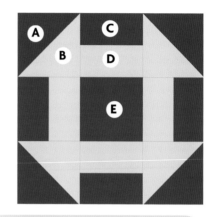

HOW IT'S DONE

1 Cut the patches as shown above based on the desired finished block size.

2 With A and B squares, follow directions for Half-Square triangles as provided in Question 147 in Chapter 11. Make two sets.

3 Layer (1) rectangle C with (1) rectangle (D), right sides together. Sew along one edge, press seam to darker fabric. Repeat (3) more times.

4 Arrange the patches as shown above. Sew rows as follows:

- Row 1: AB, CD, AB
- Row 2: CD, E, CD
- Row 3: AB, CD, AB

5 Sew Row 2 to Row 1. Sew Row 3 to Row 2. Press seams to block's outside edge.

PATCH	No	6"	9"	12"	15"	
A	2	2 7/8"	3 7/8"	4 7/8"	5 7/8"	◻
B	2	2 7/8"	3 7/8"	4 7/8"	5 7/8"	◻
C	4	1 ½" X 2 ½"	2" x 3 ½"	2 ½" x 4 ½"	3" x 5 ½"	◻
D	4	1 ½" X 2 ½"	2" x 3 ½"	2 ½" x 4 ½"	3" x 5 ½"	◻
E	1	2 ½"	3 ½"	4 ½"	5 ½"	◻

Question 23:
What is a Friendship Star block?

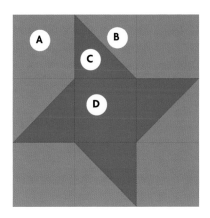

This is another example of a simple Nine-Patch variation used to teach beginners how to piece squares with Half-Square triangle units. The star appears to spin around the center square.

HOW IT'S DONE

1 Cut the patches as shown above based on the desired finished block size.

2 With B and C squares, follow directions for Half-Square triangles as provided in Question 147 in Chapter 11. Make two sets.

3 Arrange the patches as shown above. Sew rows as follows:

- Row 1: A, BC, A
- Row 2: BC, D, BC
- Row 3: A, BC, A

4 Sew Row 2 to Row 1. Sew Row 3 to Row 2. Press seams to block's outside edge.

PATCH	No	6"	9"	12"	15"	
A	4	2 1/2"	3 1/2"	4 1/2"	5 1/2"	■
B	2	2 7/8"	3 7/8"	4 7/8"	5 7/8"	■
C	2	2 7/8"	3 7/8"	4 7/8"	5 7/8"	■
D	1	2 1/2"	3 1/2"	4 1/2"	5 1/2"	■

Question 24:
What is a Birds in the Air block?

This block is similar to the Northwinds block on the opposite page, but is simpler to construct with fewer half-square triangles.

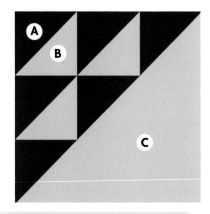

HOW IT'S DONE

1 Cut the patches as shown above based on the desired finished block size.

2 With A and B squares, follow directions for Half-Square triangles as provided in Question 147 in Chapter 11. Make two sets. You'll have (4) Half-Square AB units when done, but you only need (3). Save the remaining AB unit for another block.

3 From the last two A patches, cut each along diagonal from corner to corner, making (4) triangles. You will only need (3) triangles. Save the remaining for another block.

4 Sew the pieced triangle section in 3 rows as follows and press rows in alternating directions:
- Row 1: AB, AB, A
- Row 2: AB, A
- Row 3: A

5 Sew 3 rows together following the illustration for placement. Press.

6 Sew C triangle as shown to the pieced triangle section. Press seam to C.

PATCH	No	6"	9"	12"	15"
A	4	2 7/8"	3 7/8"	4 7/8"	5 7/8"
B	2	2 7/8"	3 7/8"	4 7/8"	5 7/8"
C	1*	4 7/8"	6 7/8"	8 7/8"	10 7/8"

*There will be 1 extra triangle once these have been cut.

Question 25:
What is a Northwinds Block?

This block has a dark side and a light side bisected on the diagonal, which gives visual movement to the design, like the wind moving across a field of wheat.

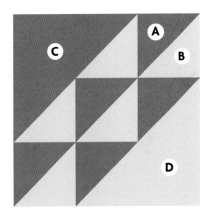

HOW IT'S DONE

1 Cut the patches as shown above based on the desired finished block size.

2 Layer (1) square A with (1) square B, right sides together with the lighter square on top. Draw a diagonal line on top square from corner to corner.

3 Sew one ¼ inch seam along one side of drawn line. (This differs from previous instructions for Half-Square triangles.)

4 Cut along drawn line (make one half square triangle unit and one loose triangle in each color) and press unit's seam to darker patch.

5 Repeat (2) more times with additional A and B patches. You'll have (3) Half-Square AB units when done, (3) loose A triangles, and (3) loose B triangles. You only need (2) loose triangles in each color.

6 Sew the center triangle section in 3 rows as follows and press rows in alternating directions:
- Row 1: B triangle, AB
- Row 2: B triangle, AB, A triangle
- Row 3: AB, A triangle

7 Sew 3 rows together following the illustration for placement. Press.

8 Sew C and D triangles as shown to the center triangle section. Press seams to larger triangles.

PATCH	No	6"	9"	12"	15"	
A	3*	2 7/8"	3 7/8"	4 7/8"	5 7/8"	
B	3*	2 7/8"	3 7/8"	4 7/8"	5 7/8"	
C	1*	4 7/8"	6 7/8"	8 7/8"	10 7/8"	
D	1*	4 7/8"	6 7/8"	8 7/8"	10 7/8"	

*There will be 1 extra triangle once these have been cut.

Question 26:

What is a Twin Star block?

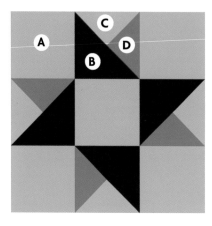

This block has a combination of Half-Square triangles and Quarter-Square triangle units to create a star that looks like two Friendship Star blocks spinning in opposite directions.

HOW IT'S DONE

1 Cut the patches as shown based on the desired finished block size.

2 Follow directions for Quarter-Square triangles as provided in Question 149 in Chapter 13. Make (4) sets.

3 Arrange the patches as shown above. Sew rows as follows:
- Row 1: A, BCD, A
- Row 2: BCD, A, BCD
- Row 3: A, BCD, A

4 Sew Row 2 to Row 1. Sew Row 3 to Row 2. Press seams to block's outside edge.

PATCH	No	6"	9"	12"	15"	
A	5	2 1/2"	3 1/2"	4 1/2"	5 1/2"	
B	2	2 7/8"	3 7/8"	4 7/8"	5 7/8"	
C	1	3 1/4"	4 1/4"	5 1/4"	6 1/4"	
D	1	3 1/4"	4 1/4"	5 1/4"	6 1/4"	

Question 27:
What is a Garden Square block?

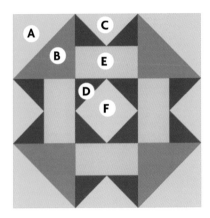

This block is reminiscent of mosaic tile floor patterns.

HOW IT'S DONE

1 Cut the patches as shown based on the desired finished block size.

2 With A and B squares, follow directions for Half-Square triangles as provided in Question 147 in Chapter 11. Make two sets. You'll have (4) Half-Square AB units when done.

3 Using square D and rectangle C, follow directions for Flying Geese blocks as provided in Question 146 in Chapter 11. Make (4) CD Flying Geese units.

4 Place E rectangle on CD Flying Geese unit, right sides together. Stitch along edge with D triangles facing out, as shown above. Press seam to E. Repeat (3) more times.

5 To make center square, place square D in corner of square F, follow directions for Square in a Square block as provided in Question 152 in Chapter 11.

6 Arrange the patches as shown above. Sew rows as follows:
• Row 1: AB, CDE, AB
• Row 2: CDE, DF, CDE
• Row 3: AB, CDE, AB

7 Sew Row 2 to Row 1. Sew Row 3 to Row 2. Press seams to block's outside edge.

PATCH	No	6"	9"	12"	15"
A	2	2 7/8"	3 7/8"	4 7/8"	5 7/8"
B	2	2 7/8"	3 7/8"	4 7/8"	5 7/8"
C	4	1 1/2" X 2 1/2"	2" X 3 1/2"	2 1/2" X 4 1/2"	3" X 5 1/2"
D	12	1 1/2"	2"	2 1/2"	3"
E	4	1 1/2" X 2 1/2"	2" X 3 1/2"	2 1/2" X 4 1/2"	3" X 5 1/2"
F	1	2 1/2"	3 1/2"	4 1/2"	5 1/2"

Question 28:

What is a Dove in the Window block?

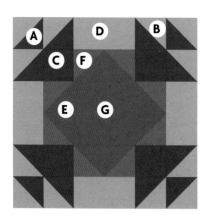

This traditional block probably gets its name because it looks like a dove flying past a window as spring approaches.

PATCH	No	6"	9"	12"	15"
A	2	1 7/8"	2 3/8"	2 7/8"	3 3/8"
B	6	1 7/8"	2 3/8"	2 7/8"	3 3/8"
C	2	2 7/8"	3 7/8"	4 7/8"	5 7/8"
D	4	1 1/2" X 2 1/2"	2" X 3 1/2"	2 1/2" X 4 1/2"	3" X 5 1/2"
E	4	1 1/2" X 2 1/2"	2" X 3 1/2"	2 1/2" X 4 1/2"	3" X 5 1/2"
F	8	1 1/2"	2"	2 1/2"	3"
G	1	2 1/2"	3 1/2"	4 1/2"	5 1/2"

HOW IT'S DONE

1 Cut the patches as shown based on the desired finished block size.

2 With A and B squares, follow directions for Half-Square triangles as provided in Question 147 in Chapter 11. Make two sets. You'll have (4) Half-Square AB units when done.

3 With remaining (2) B squares, draw line diagonally through middle and cut in half. Sew B triangles to each A side of AB Half-Square triangle units. Press seams to B triangles.

4 On C patch, draw line diagonally through middle and cut in half. Sew C triangle to B/AB/B unit per diagram. Press seam to C triangle. Repeat once more.

5 Using square F and rectangle E, follow directions for Flying Geese Blocks as provided in Question 146 in Chapter 11. Make (4) EF Flying Geese units.

6 Place D rectangle on EF Flying Geese unit, right sides together. Stitch along edge with F triangles facing out, as shown above. Press seam to D. Repeat (3) more times.

7 Arrange the patches as shown above. Sew rows as follows:
- Row 1: B/AB/B/C, E/F/D, B/AB/B/C
- Row 2: E/F/D, G, E/F/D
- Row 3: B/AB/B/C, E/F/D, B/AB/B/C

8 Sew Row 2 to Row 1. Sew Row 3 to Row 2. Press seams to block's outside edge.

Question 29:
What is a Maple Leaf block?

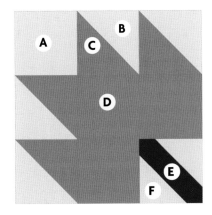

This block looks like a leaf that has drifted to the ground on an autumn day, hence the name. (The stem is sometimes added to the square in the corner; this is optional.)

HOW IT'S DONE

1 Cut the patches as shown based on the desired finished block size.

2 With B and C squares, follow directions for Half-Square triangles as provided in Question 147 in Chapter 11. Make two sets. You'll have (4) Half-Square BC units when done.

3 To make the stem unit, place square F in corner of square E, matching outer two edges of F and E. Draw diagonal line from outer corner to outer corner of F. Sew along line, creating a Half-Square triangle.

4 Check for accuracy, then trim triangle seam to ¼ inch.

5 Open triangle and press seam to outer corner.

6 Repeat in opposite corner of E.

7 Arrange the patches as shown above. Sew rows as follows:
- Row 1: A, BC, BC
- Row 2: BC, D, D
- Row 3: BC, D, EFF

8 Sew Row 2 to Row 1. Sew Row 3 to Row 2. Press seams to block's outside edge.

PATCH	No	6"	9"	12"	15"	
A	1	2 ½"	3 ½"	4 ½"	5 ½"	□
B	2	2 ⅞"	3 ⅞"	4 ⅞"	5 ⅞"	□
C	2	2 ⅞"	3 ⅞"	4 ⅞"	5 ⅞"	□
D	3	2 ½"	3 ½"	4 ½"	5 ½"	□
E	1	2 ½"	3 ½"	4 ½"	5 ½"	□
F	2	2 ½"	3 ½"	4 ½"	5 ½"	□

Question 30:
What is a Fifty-Four Forty or Fight block?

This block takes its name from a land dispute between Great Britain and the United States over the Oregon Territory back in the 1840s. "Fifty-Four Forty" refers to the 54°40' longitudinal line west of the Rocky Mountains that was the disputed border. The dispute was resolved with the Treaty of Oregon in 1846.

HOW IT'S DONE

1 Cut the patches as shown based on the desired finished block size.

2 With squares A and B, follow directions for Four-Patch blocks as provided in Question 145 in Chapter 11. Make (4) AB Four-Patch units.

3 Sew the triangle units cut from templates, D to C and E to C, as shown in illustration. Press seams to D and E. Repeat (3) more times to create (4) triangle units.

4 Arrange the patches as shown above. Sew rows as follows:
• Row 1: AB Four-Patch, CDE, AB Four-Patch
• Row 2: CDE, AB Four-Patch, CDE
• Row 3: AB Four-Patch, CDE, AB Four-Patch

5 Sew Row 2 to Row 1. Sew Row 3 to Row 2. Press seams to block's outside edge.

PATCH	No	6"	9"	12"	15"	
A	10	1 ½"	2"	2 ½"	3"	■
B	10	1 ½"	2"	2 ½"	3"	■
C*	4	2 ½"	3 ½"	4 ½"	5 ½"	▲
D*	4	2 ½"	3 ½"	4 ½"	5 ½"	▲
E*	4	2 ½"	3 ½"	4 ½"	5 ½"	▲

*Cut shapes using templates provided, cut strips the width described in the table above. Please note that E is a reverse of D.

Question 31:
What is a Road to Paradise block?

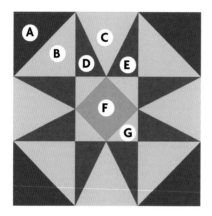

This block uses the same type of star points as the Fifty-Four Forty or Fight block, but the corners and center are different. Many blocks are named for Bible stories or characters, which is understandable given that so many of these traditional patchwork blocks were designed by American women in earlier times.

PATCH	No	6"	9"	12"	15"
A	2	2 7/8"	3 7/8"	4 7/8"	5 7/8"
B	2	2 7/8"	3 7/8"	4 7/8"	5 7/8"
C*	4	3"	4"	5"	6"
D*	4	2 1/2" X 3"	3 1/2" X 4"	4 1/2" X 5"	5 1/2" X 6"
E*	4	2 1/2" X 3"	3 1/2" X 4"	4 1/2" X 5"	5 1/2" X 6"
F	1	2 1/2"	3 1/2"	4 1/2"	5 1/2"
G	4	1 1/2"	2"	2 1/2"	3"

*Cut patches C, D, and E from templates in the back of this book. Be sure patch E is a reverse of patch D. They all may be cut from fabric scraps described in the table above.

HOW IT'S DONE

1 Cut the patches as shown based on the desired finished block size.

2 Layer (1) square A with (1) square B, right sides together with the lighter square on top.

3 Draw a diagonal line on top square from corner to corner.

4 Sew two ¼ inch seams along both sides of drawn line.

5 Cut along drawn line (makes two Half-Square triangle units) and press each unit's seam to darker patch.

6 Repeat (1) more time with additional A and B patches. You'll have (4) Half-Square AB units when done.

7 For the triangle units, sew the units cut from templates, D to C and E to C, as shown in illustration. Press seams to D and E. Repeat (3) more times to create (4) triangle units.

8 For the center unit, place square G in corner of larger square F, matching outer two edges of G and F. Draw diagonal line from outer corner to outer corner of G. Sew along line, creating a Half-Square triangle.

9 Check for accuracy then trim triangle seam to ¼ inch.

10 Open triangle and press seam to outer corner.

11 Repeat in remaining 3 corners of square F.

12 Arrange the patches as shown above. Sew rows as follows:
• Row 1: AB, CDE, AB
• Row 2: CDE, FG, CDE
• Row 3: AB, CDE, AB

13 Sew Row 2 to Row 1. Sew Row 3 to Row 2. Press seams to block's outside edge.

Question 32:
What is a Card Trick block?

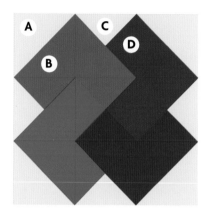

This block looks like four playing cards fanned out on a table. It contains Half-Square triangle and Quarter-Square triangle units. There are many bias edges, so take care in piecing this block.

PATCH	No	6"	9"	12"	15"
A	4	2 7/8"	3 7/8"	4 7/8"	5 7/8"
B	1 ea.	2 7/8"	3 7/8"	4 7/8"	5 7/8"
C	1	3 1/4"	4 1/4"	5 1/4"	6 1/4"
D	1 ea.	3 1/4"	4 1/4"	5 1/4"	6 1/4"

HOW IT'S DONE

1 Cut the patches as shown based on the desired finished block size.

2 For the Half-Square triangles, layer (1) square A with (1) square B, right sides together with the lighter square on top.

3 Draw a diagonal line on top square from corner to corner.

4 Sew one ¼ inch seam along one side of drawn line. (This differs from previous instructions for Half-Square triangles.)

5 Cut along drawn line (make one Half-Square triangle unit and one loose triangle in each color) and press unit's seam to darker patch.

6 Repeat (3) more times with additional A and B patches. You'll have (4) Half-Square AB units when done, one in each B color, (4) loose A triangles and (4) loose B triangles. You only need the B triangles.

7 For BCD Quarter-Square triangles, follow directions for Quarter-Square triangles as provided in Question 149 in Chapter 11. Make (4) sets.

8 For center Quarter-Square triangle, sew a pair of different D color triangles together, following illustration for color placement. Press seams to darker fabric. Repeat with remaining different D color triangles. Then, sew two pairs together, again following illustration for color placement.

9 Arrange the patches as shown above. Sew rows as follows:
- Row 1: AB, BCD, AB
- Row 2: BCD, DDDD, BCD
- Row 3: AB, BCD, AB

10 Sew Row 2 to Row 1. Sew Row 3 to Row 2. Press seams toward block's outside edge.

Question 33:
What is a Variable Star block?

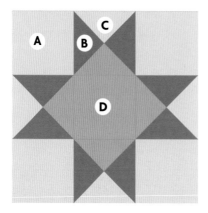

One of the most common star blocks is the Variable Star. It uses Flying Geese units to make the star points and is an example of an uneven Nine-Patch.

HOW IT'S DONE

1 Cut the patches as shown based on the desired finished block size.

2 With square B and rectangle C, follow directions for Flying Geese blocks as provided in Question 146 in Chapter 11.

3 Arrange the patches as shown. Sew rows as follows:
- Row 1: A, BC, A
- Row 2: BC, D, BC
- Row 3: A, BC, A

4 Sew Row 2 to Row 1. Sew Row 3 to Row 2. Press seams to block's outside edge.

PATCH	No	6"	9"	12"	15"
A	4	2"	2 ¾"	3 ½"	4 ¼"
B	8	2"	2 ¾"	3 ½"	4 ¼"
C	4	2" X 3 ½"	2 ¾" X 5"	3 ½" X 6 ½"	4 ½" X 8"
D	1	3 ½"	5"	6 ½"	8"

Question 34:
What is a Cat's Cradle block?

This is a variation on a Hatchet block or a Double X block. While it's not quite a Star block, it shares many of the same characteristics.

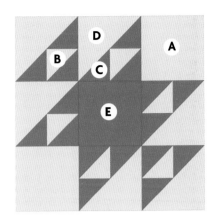

HOW IT'S DONE

1 Cut the patches as shown based on the desired finished block size.

2 With B and C squares, follow directions for Half-Square triangles as provided in Question 147 in Chapter 11. Make (3) sets.

3 With remaining (6) C squares, draw line diagonally through middle and cut in half. Sew C triangles to each B side of BC Half-Square triangle units. Press seams to C triangles.

4 On D patch, draw line diagonally through middle and cut in half. Sew D triangle to C/BC/C unit per diagram. Press seam to D triangle. Repeat (5) more times.

5 Arrange the patches as shown above. Sew rows as follows:
- Row 1: BCD, BCD, A
- Row 2: BCD, E, BCD
- Row 3: A, BCD, BCD

6 Sew Row 2 to Row 1. Sew Row 3 to Row 2. Press seams toward block's outside edge.

PATCH	No	6"	9"	12"	15"
A	2	2 1/2"	3 1/2"	4 1/2"	5 1/2"
B	3	1 7/8"	2 3/8"	2 7/8"	3 3/8"
C	9	1 7/8"	2 3/8"	2 7/8"	3 3/8"
D	3	2 7/8"	3 7/8"	4 7/8"	5 7/8"
E	1	2 1/2"	3 1/2"	4 1/2"	5 1/2"

35 What is a Storm at Sea block?

36 What is a Basket block?

37 Are there variations on the Basket block?

38 What is a Sawtooth Star block?

39 What is a Contrary Wife block?

40 What is an Irish Chain block?

41 What is a Crown of Thorns?

42 What is a King's Crown block?

43 What is a Snowball block?

44 What is a Drunkard's Path block?

45 What is a Solomon's Puzzle block?

SIXTEEN-PATCH
BLOCKS

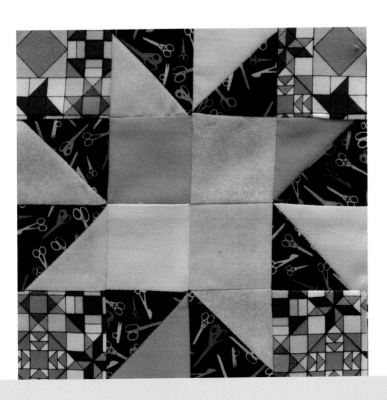

Question 35:
What is a Storm at Sea block?

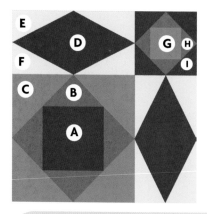

This block has many triangles and diamonds, which make it look like the ripple of waves on water. To construct this block, each section will be made separately and then joined to the others.

HOW IT'S DONE

1 Cut the patches as shown based on the desired finished block size.

2 For ABC unit, cut B patch across both diagonals, corner to corner, creating (4) Quarter-Square triangles. Cut C patch across one diagonal, corner to corner, creating (2) Half-Square triangles. Repeat on second C patch for (4) total Half-Square triangles.

3 Follow directions for Square in a Square block as provided in Question 152 in Chapter 11.

4 For GHI unit, cut H patch across both diagonals, corner to corner, creating (4) Quarter-Square triangles. Cut I patch across one diagonal, corner to corner, creating (2) Half-Square triangles. Repeat on second I patch for (4) total Half-Square triangles.

5 Follow directions for Square in a Square block as provided in Question 152.

6 For DEF unit, sew (2) E triangles along opposite sides of D diamond. Press seams to E. Sew (2) F triangles along opposite sides of D diamond. Press seams to F. Repeat for second DEF unit.

7 Arrange the patches as shown above. Sew rows as follows:
• Row 1: DEF, GHI
• Row 2: ABC, DEF

8 Sew Row 2 to Row 1. Press seams toward block's outside edge.

PATCH	No	6"	9"	12"	15"
A	1	2 1/2"	3 1/2"	4 1/2"	5 1/2"
B	1	3 1/4"	4 1/4"	5 1/4"	6 1/4"
C	2	2 7/8"	3 7/8"	4 7/8"	5 7/8"
D	2	2 1/4" X 2 7/8"	3 1/8" X 4"	4 1/8" X 5 1/8"	5" X 6 1/4"
E*	2	1 5/8" X 3 1/4"	2 1/8" X 4 1/4"	2 5/8" X 5 1/4"	3 1/8" X 6 1/4"
F*	2	1 5/8" X 3 1/4"	2 1/8" X 4 1/4"	2 5/8" X 5 1/4"	3 1/8" X 6 1/4"
G	1	1 1/2"	2"	2 1/2"	3"
H	1	2 1/4"	2 3/4"	3 1/4"	3 3/4"
I	2	1 7/8"	2 3/8"	2 7/8"	3 3/8"

*Patches E and F are cut from a rectangle the size given and then cut into a triangle. Be sure that patch F is a reverse of patch E.

Question 36:
What is a Basket block?

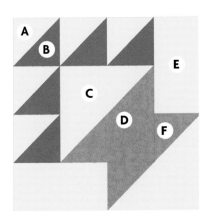

There are several types of basket blocks; they may be left empty or "filled" with any number of appliquéd items such as flowers, eggs, fruit, or animals. One example is given. This basket is empty and the triangles represent the handle.

HOW IT'S DONE

1 Cut the patches as shown based on the desired finished block size.

2 With A and B squares, follow directions for Half-Square triangles as provided in Question 147 in Chapter 11. Make (3) sets.

3 For CD unit, layer (1) square C with (1) square D, right sides together with the lighter square on top.

4 Draw a diagonal line on top square from corner to corner.

5 Sew one ¼ inch seam along one side of drawn line.

6 Cut along drawn line (makes one Half-Square triangle unit, one loose C triangle and one loose D triangle) and press the unit's seam to darker patch. Save the loose C triangle.

7 Cut F patch across one diagonal, corner to corner, creating (2) Half-Square triangles.

8 Sew triangle F triangle to rectangle E. Press to F. Repeat on second EF set.

9 Carefully following illustration as a guide, sew (3) AB units together. Press seams in one direction. These will be the basket's top. Then, sew (2) AB units together for the side, as shown in illustration. Press seam in one direction. Sew the AB pair to CD. Press seam. Sew (3) AB units to the AB/CD unit. Press seam.

10 Sew (2) EF units to either side of the ABCD unit, following illustration. Press seams to the block's outside. Sew C triangle to corner of block. Press seam to C.

PATCH	No	6"	9"	12"	15"
A	3	2 ³/₈"	3 ¹/₈"	3 ⁷/₈"	4 ⁵/₈"
B	3	2 ³/₈"	3 ¹/₈"	3 ⁷/₈"	4 ⁵/₈"
C	2	3 ⁷/₈"	5 ³/₈"	6 ⁷/₈"	8 ³/₈"
D	1	3 ⁷/₈"	5 ³/₈"	6 ⁷/₈"	8 ³/₈"
E	2	2" X 3 ½"	2 ¾" X 5"	3 ½" X 6 ½"	4 ¼" X 8"
F	1	2 ³/₈"	3 ¹/₈"	3 ⁷/₈"	4 ⁵/₈"

Question 37:
Are there variations on the Basket block?

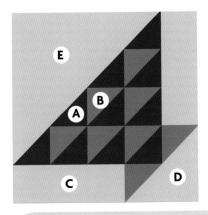

There are so many variations on the Basket block that we wanted to offer another version. This is a simple basket with no handle, and again, you can "fill" it with appliquéd flowers, or a handle could be added. Internet searches and block encyclopedias will give you still more basket patterns. Consider a basket sampler quilt as a future project.

HOW IT'S DONE

1 Cut the patches as shown based on the desired finished block size.

2 With A and B squares, follow directions for Half-Square triangles as provided in Question 147 in Chapter 11. Make (3) sets.

3 From the remaining two A patches and one B patch, cut each in half diagonally, corner to corner, to create a total of (4) A triangles and (2) B triangles.

4 Sew the basket by arranging the triangles and Half-Square triangles units as shown above. Sew rows as follows and press seams for each row in alternating directions:

- Row 1: A triangle
- Row 2: A triangle, AB
- Row 3: A triangle, AB, AB
- Row 4: A triangle, AB, AB, AB

5 Sew rows together. Press seams in one direction.

6 Sew triangle B triangle to C rectangle. Press to B. Repeat on second BC set.

7 Sew BC units to either side of AB basket, as shown.

8 Sew triangles D and E to opposite corners of the basket to complete block. Press seams toward triangles.

PATCH	No	6"	9"	12"	15"
A	5	2"	2 5/8"	3 1/4"	3 7/8"
B	4	2"	2 5/8"	3 1/4"	3 7/8"
C	2	1 3/4" X 4 1/8"	2 1/4" X 5 7/8"	2 7/8" X 7 3/4"	3 1/2" X 9 1/2"
D*	1	3 1/4"	4 1/2"	5 5/8"	6 7/8"
E*	1	5 5/8"	8"	10 1/2"	12 7/8"

*When cutting the square for D and E, there will be one triangle left over.

Question 38:

What is a Sawtooth Star block?

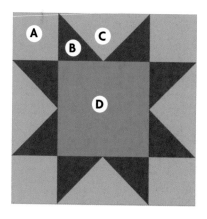

One of the most common star blocks is the Sawtooth Star. It uses Flying Geese units to make the star points and is an example of an uneven Nine-Patch.

HOW IT'S DONE

1 Cut the patches as shown based on the desired finished block size.

2 With B square and C rectangle, follow directions for Flying Geese blocks as provided in Question 146 in Chapter 11.

3 Arrange the patches as shown above. Sew rows as follows:
- Row 1: A, BC, A
- Row 2: BC, D, BC
- Row 3: A, BC, A

4 Sew Row 2 to Row 1. Sew Row 3 to Row 2. Press seams to block's outside edge.

PATCH	No	6"	9"	12"	15"
A	4	2"	2 3/4"	3 1/2"	4 1/4"
B	8	2"	2 3/4"	3 1/2"	4 1/4"
C	4	2" X 3 1/2"	2 3/4" X 5"	3 1/2" X 6 1/2"	4 1/2" X 8"
D	1	3 1/2"	5"	6 1/2"	8"

Question 39:
What is a Contrary Wife block?

Don't you just love the name of this block? Maybe it gets its name from all of the triangles that head in opposing directions. (You'll need a sense of humor to make this block!)

HOW IT'S DONE

1 Cut the patches as shown above based on the desired finished block size.

2 With B and C squares, follow directions for Half-Square triangles as provided in Question 147 in Chapter 11. Make (8) sets.

3 With B square and D rectangle, follow directions for Flying Geese blocks as provided in Question 146 in Chapter 11. Make (4) sets.

4 Sew (2) BC units to each side of BD Flying Geese unit. Finish unit is BC, BD, BC. Repeat (3) more times.

5 Cut patch G in half, twice, along the diagonal, forming an X cut.

6 Sew long edge of G triangle to side of F patch. Press seam to G and repeat (3) more times.

7 Cut patch E in half, once, along the diagonal. Repeat once creating (4) triangles.

8 Sew long edge of E triangle to side of FG patch. Press seam to E and repeat (3) more times.

9 Arrange the patches as shown above. Sew rows as follows:
- Row 1: A, BCBDBC, A
- Row 2: BCBDBC, EFG, BCBDBC
- Row 3: A, BCBDBC, A

10 Sew Row 2 to Row 1. Sew Row 3 to Row 2. Press seams to block's outside edge.

PATCH	No	6"	9"	12"	15"	
A	4	1 ½"	2"	2 ½"	3"	
B	8	1 ⅞"	2 ⅜"	2 ⅞"	3 ⅜"	☐
C	4	1 ⅞"	2 ⅜"	2 ⅞"	3 ⅜"	☐
D	4	1 ½" X 2 ½"	2" X 3 ½"	2 ½" X 4 ½"	3" X 5 ½"	▭
E	2	2 ⅞"	3 ⅞"	4 ⅞"	5 ⅞"	☐
F	1	2 ½"	3 ½"	4 ½"	5 ½"	☐
G	1	3 ¼"	4 ¼"	5 ¼"	6 ¼"	☐

Question 40:
What is an Irish Chain block?

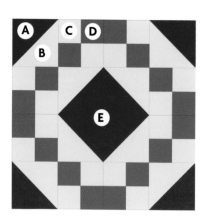

Traditionally, this block is made in hues of green, but it looks great in many other colors and patterns too. It can be used by itself or as an alternating block in a quilt. When used as an alternating block, it creates a secondary pattern, and is a unique way to set blocks and show them off both as individuals and part of an overall design.

PATCH	No	6"	9"	12"	15"	
A	2	2 ⅜"	3 ⅛"	3 ⅞"	4 ⅝"	☐
B	4	2 ⅜"	3 ⅛"	3 ⅞"	4 ⅝"	☐
C	16	1 ¼"	1 ⅝"	2"	2 ⅜"	☐
D	16	1 ¼"	1 ⅝"	2"	2 ⅜"	☐
E	1	2 ⅝"	3 ⅝"	4 ¾"	5 ¼"	☐

HOW IT'S DONE

1 Cut the patches as shown based on the desired finished block size.

2 With A and B squares, follow directions for Half-Square triangles as provided in Question 147 in Chapter 11. Make (4) sets.

3 With C and D squares, follow directions for Four-Patch blocks as provided in Question 145 in Chapter 11. Make (8) sets.

4 With B and E squares, follow directions for Square in a Square block as provided in Question 152 in Chapter 11.

5 Arrange the patches as shown above. Sew rows as follows:
- Row 1: AB, CD pair, AB
- Row 2: CD pair, BE, CD pair
- Row 3: AB, CD pair, AB

6 Sew Row 2 to Row 1. Sew Row 3 to Row 2. Press seams to block's outside edge.

Question 41:

What is a Crown of Thorns?

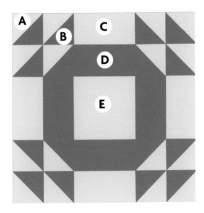

This patchwork block evokes memories of the crown of thorns that Jesus wore on the cross. It is a traditional block from early America.

PATCH	No	6"	9"	12"	15"	
A	8	1 7/8"	2 3/8"	2 7/8"	3 3/8"	■
B	8	1 7/8"	2 3/8"	2 7/8"	3 3/8"	■
C	4	1 1/2" X 2 1/2"	2" X 3 1/2"	2 1/2" X 4 1/2"	3" X 5 1/2"	□
D	4	1 1/2" X 2 1/2"	2" X 3 1/2"	2 1/2" X 4 1/2"	3" X 5 1/2"	□
E	1	2 1/2"	3 1/2"	4 1/2"	5 1/2"	■

HOW IT'S DONE

1 Cut the patches as shown above based on the desired finished block size.

2 With A and B squares, follow directions for Half-Square triangles as provided in Question 147 in Chapter 11. Make (8) sets.

3 Arrange (4) sets of AB units into a Four-Patch unit as shown above and follow directions for Four-Patch blocks as provided in Question 145 in Chapter 11.

4 Place C rectangle on D rectangle, right sides together. Stitch along edge. Press seam to darker fabric. Repeat (3) more times.

5 Arrange the patches as shown above. Sew rows as follows:
• Row 1: AB Four-Patch, CD, AB Four-Patch
• Row 2: CD, E, CD
• Row 3: AB Four-Patch, CD, AB Four-Patch

6 Sew Row 2 to Row 1. Sew Row 3 to Row 2. Press seams to block's outside edge.

Question 42:
What is a King's Crown block?

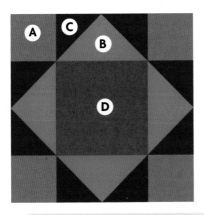

Similar to a Sawtooth Star block, the King's Crown block has its Flying Geese units inverted. This makes the points look like a crown with its tips touching.

HOW IT'S DONE

1 Cut the patches as shown above based on the desired finished block size.

2 With C square and B rectangle, follow directions for Flying Geese blocks as provided in Question 146 in Chapter 11. Make (4) Flying Geese units.

3 Arrange the patches as shown above. Sew rows as follows:
- Row 1: A, BC, A
- Row 2: BC, D, BC
- Row 3: A, BC, A

4 Sew Row 2 to Row 1. Sew Row 3 to Row 2. Press seams to block's outside edge.

PATCH	No	6"	9"	12"	15"	
A	4	2"	2 3/4"	3 1/2"	4 1/4"	
B	4	2" X 3 1/2"	2 3/4" X 5"	3 1/2" X 6 1/2"	4 1/4" X 8"	
C	4	2 3/8"	3 1/8"	3 7/8"	4 5/8"	
D	1	3 1/2"	5"	6 1/2"	8"	

Question 43:
What is a Snowball block?

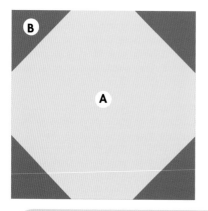

The Snowball block gives the optical illusion of a round shape when arranged with other patchwork blocks. The corners can be trimmed to other sizes to work this into the design or to align the block's seams with adjacent blocks. The Snowball block is also an excellent block to use in friendship quilts as there is plenty of room to write or embroider thoughts and names.

HOW IT'S DONE

1 Cut the patches as shown based on the desired finished block size.

2 Place square B on corner of square A, matching outer two edges of A and B. Draw diagonal line from outer corner to outer corner of B. Sew along line.

3 Check for accuracy, then trim seam to ¼ inch.

4 Open triangle and press seam toward outer corner.

5 Repeat steps 1 to 4 on other (3) corners.

PATCH	No	6"	9"	12"	15"
A	1	6 ½"	9 ½"	12 ½"	15 ½"
B	4	2 ½"	3 ½"	4 ½"	5 ½"

Question 44:
What is a Drunkard's Path block?

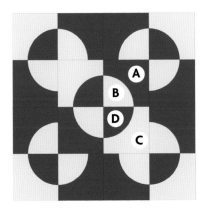

This block has been popular since the temperance movement in the United States in the 1920s and '30s. It served to poke fun at or discourage drunkenness. This block uses the same piecing technique as the Solomon's Puzzle block, although the orientation of the patches is different.

HOW IT'S DONE

1 Cut the patches and template pieces as shown based on the desired finished block size.

2 With right sides together sew B to A matching centers and ends. Press each side outward. Repeat (9) more times to make 10 units. To sew curves, have the concave patch on top and the convex patch underneath. Sew slowly and continue aligning pieces while you sew.

3 Sew D to C matching centers and ends. Press each side outward. Repeat (5) more times to make 6 units.

4 Arrange the patches as shown above paying careful attention to the orientation of each unit. Sew rows as follows:
- Row 1: CD, AB, AB, CD
- Row 2: AB, CD, AB, AB
- Row 3: AB, AB, CD, AB
- Row 4: CD, AB, AB, CD

5 Sew Row 2 to Row 1. Sew Row 3 to Row 2. Sew Row 4 to Row 3.

6 Press seams.

PATCH	No	6"	9"	12"	15"
A	10	2"	2 ¾"	3 ½"	4 ½"
B	10	2"	2 ¾"	3 ½"	4 ½"
C	6	2"	2 ¾"	3 ½"	4 ½"
D	6	2"	2 ¾"	3 ½"	4 ½"

Question 45:

What is a Solomon's Puzzle block?

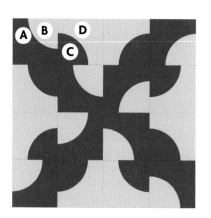

Solomon's Puzzle is a variation of the Drunkard's Path block. Its name comes from the Bible story about Solomon's dilemma. These patches are made from templates but may be cut from the sizes of the squares listed in the table below.

PATCH	No	6"	9"	12"	15"
A	8	2"	2 ¾"	3 ½"	4 ½"
B	8	2"	2 ¾"	3 ½"	4 ½"
C	8	2"	2 ¾"	3 ½"	4 ½"
D	8	2"	2 ¾"	3 ½"	4 ½"

HOW IT'S DONE

1 Cut the patches and template pieces as shown based on the desired finished block size.

2 With right sides together, sew B to A matching centers and ends. Press each side outward. Repeat (7) more times to make 8 units. To sew curves, have the concave patch on top and the convex patch underneath. Sew slowly and continue aligning pieces while you sew.

3 Sew D to C matching centers and ends. Press each side outward. Repeat (7) more times to make 8 units.

4 Arrange the patches as shown above paying careful attention to the orientation of each unit. Sew rows as follows:
- Row 1: AB, CD, CD, AB
- Row 2: CD, AB, AB, CD
- Row 3: CD, AB, AB, CD
- Row 4: AB, CD, CD, AB

5 Sew Row 2 to Row 1. Sew Row 3 to Row 2. Sew Row 4 to Row 3.

6 Press seams.

46 What is Jacob's Ladder block?

47 What is a Pine Tree block?

48 What is a Heart block?

49 What is a Handy Andy block?

50 What is a Lady of the Lake block?

51 What is a Monkey Wrench block?

52 What is a Snail's Trail block?

53 What is a Virginia Reel block?

54 What is a House block?

55 What is a Delectable Mountains block?

56 What is a Bridal Path block?

57 What is a Dutch Rose block?

5
THIRTY-SIX AND SIXTY-FOUR PATCH BLOCKS

Question 46:
What is Jacob's Ladder block?

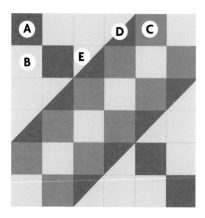

This block looks like it has an ascending staircase, like the ladder by which Jacob traveled into Heaven in the Bible story.

HOW IT'S DONE

1 Cut the patches and template pieces as shown above based on the desired finished block size.

2 For the Four-Patch units AB and BC, top row, sew (4) AB and (6) BC units. You can chain piece these rows. Press seams to darker fabrics.

3 Sew top rows to bottom rows as shown above. You'll have (2) AB Four-Patch units and (3) BC Four-Patch units. Press the blocks with the seams going to one side — doesn't matter which.

4 With D and E squares, follow directions for Half-Square triangles as provided in Question 147 in Chapter 11. Make (4) sets.

5 Use the DE units to make (4) Four-Patch units with remaining B and C squares. Carefully following the illustration above to ensure the correct orientation of each patch and unit, sew B to DE for top row and DE to C for bottom row. Sew rows together. There are (4) total Four-Patch units made with the Half-Square triangles.

6 Arrange the patches as shown above. Sew rows as follows:
• Row 1: AB, BCDE, BC
• Row 2: BCDE, BC, BCDE
• Row 3: BC, BCDE, AB

7 Sew Row 2 to Row 1. Sew Row 3 to Row 2. Press seams to block's outside edge.

PATCH	No	6"	9"	12"	15"
A	4	1 1/2"	2"	2 1/2"	3"
B	14	1 1/2"	2"	2 1/2"	3"
C	10	1 1/2"	2"	2 1/2"	3"
D	4	1 7/8"	2 3/8"	2 7/8"	3 3/8"
E	4	1 7/8"	2 3/8"	2 7/8"	3 3/8"

Question 47:
What is a Pine Tree block?

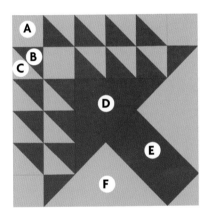

Designed to be set on-point, the Pine Tree block is traditionally made from using a single color for the leaves, but you might try it in a scrappy version with many hues of green or fall colors instead.

PATCH	No	6"	9"	12"	15"
A	4	1 1/2"	2"	2 1/2"	3"
B	8	1 7/8"	2 3/8"	2 7/8"	3 3/8"
C*	8	1 7/8"	2 3/8"	2 7/8"	3 3/8"
D*	1	3 7/8"	5 3/8"	6 7/8"	8 3/8"
E	1	1 7/8" X 3 3/8"	2 5/8" X 4 3/4"	3 3/8" X 6 1/8"	4" X 7 1/2"
F*	1	5 1/4"	7 1/4"	9 1/4"	11 1/4"

* There will be extra triangles from these shapes.

HOW IT'S DONE

1 Cut the patches as shown based on the desired finished block size.

2 With B and C squares, follow directions for Half-Square triangles as provided in Question 147 in Chapter 11. Make (7) sets.

3 Cut remaining B and C patches in half, from corner to corner, to make (4) triangles.

4 Cut D patch in half diagonally, from corner to corner, to make (2) triangles. You will only need one for the block.

5 Assemble tree in sections. Carefully follow illustration above for color placement and patch orientation, start with tree's rows:
- Row 1: A, BC, BC, BC, BC, A
- Row 2: BC, A, BC, BC, BC, B triangle
- Sew (3) BC units together, following illustration for placement. Repeat once more.
- Row 3: (3) BC unit, (3) BC unit, D triangle.
- Row 4: A, B triangle.

6 Press rows' seams in alternating directions. Sew rows together in order.

7 Cut F patch in half diagonally, from corner to corner, to make (2) triangles.

8 Sew triangle F to one side of rectangle E. Press seam to F. Repeat on opposite side of E. Sew C triangles to E as shown in illustration.

9 Sew the CFEF unit to tree unit. Press to the CFEF unit.

Question 48:
What is a Heart block?

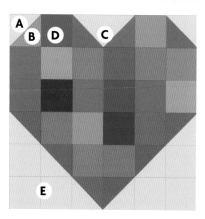

This is a fun, pieced heart shape made of several different squares of fabric. In this case, the scrappier it is, the better it will look.

HOW IT'S DONE

1 Cut the patches as shown based on the desired finished block size.

2 With A and B squares, follow directions for Half-Square triangles as provided in Question 147 in Chapter 11. Make (4) sets.

3 With B square and C rectangle, follow directions for Flying Geese blocks as provided in Question 146 in Chapter 11.

4 Carefully following illustration, arrange patches and units as shown. Sew each row, pressing seams from row to row in alternating directions. Sew rows together. Press seams.

PATCH	No	6"	9"	12"	15"
A	4	1 7/8"	2 3/8"	2 7/8"	3 3/8"
B*	6	1 7/8"	2 3/8"	2 7/8"	3 3/8"
C	1	1 7/8" X 2 1/2"	2 3/8" X 3 1/2"	2 7/8" X 6 1/2"	3 3/8" X 5 1/2"
D*	20	1 1/2"	2"	2 1/2"	3"
E	6	1 1/2"	2"	2 1/2"	3"

* Use several different fabrics for B and D.

Question 49:
What is a Handy Andy block?

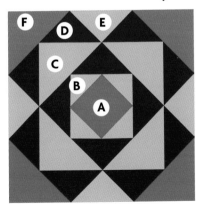

Here's another block included in part for having a great name. Handy Andy is made from a Square in a Square format, using Flying Geese units instead of triangles.

HOW IT'S DONE

1 Cut the patches as shown above based on the desired finished block size.

2 Cut B patch in half diagonally. Repeat with additional B patch to create (4) triangles.

3 Sew long edge of B triangle to side of A patch. Press seam to B and repeat (3) more times.

4 Cut D patches in half twice, along the diagonal corners to corners, forming an X cut. Repeat with remaining (2) D patches to create (12) triangles.

5 Sew long edge of D triangle to side of AB square. Press seam to D and repeat (3) more times.

6 For the Flying Geese units, please note that this is a different piecing technique used to conserve fabric. Cut (2) C patches in half diagonally to create (4) triangles.

7 Following the illustration, sew long edge of D triangle to short side of C

triangle. Press seam to D. Repeat on C's other side. Repeat (3) more times.

8 Cut E patch in half, twice, diagonally, forming an X cut.

9 Cut (2) F patches in half diagonally to create (4) triangles.

10 Carefully following illustration for placement, sew F triangle's long edge to the pointed end of Flying Geese unit. Press seam to F. Repeat (3) more times on remaining Flying Geese units.

11 Sew one F/Flying Geese unit to one side of ABD square. Press seam out to F. Repeat on opposite side of ABD square.

12 For remaining two Flying Geese units, sew E triangles to both short sides of the Flying Geese unit. Press seams to E.

13 Following illustration for placement, sew corner units to opposite side of square/Flying Geese unit. Press seams toward corners.

PATCH	No	6"	9"	12"	15"
A	1	2"	2 5/8"	3 3/8"	4"
B	2	1 7/8"	2 3/8"	2 7/8"	3 3/8"
C	2	2 7/8"	3 7/8"	4 7/8"	5 7/8"
D	3	3 1/4"	4 1/4"	5 1/4"	6 1/4"
E	1	3 1/4"	4 1/4"	5 1/4"	6 1/4"
F	2	2 7/8"	3 7/8"	4 7/8"	5 7/8"

Question 50:
What is a Lady of the Lake block?

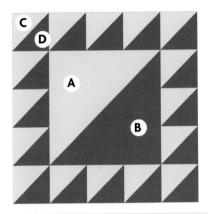

Like the Storm at Sea block, the many triangles of this block look like ripples seen on water.

HOW IT'S DONE

1 Cut the patches as shown above based on the desired finished block size.

2 For the center Half-Square triangle unit, layer square A with square B, follow directions for Half-Square triangles as provided in Question 147 in Chapter 11. You will only need one Half-Square triangle unit. Save the remaining for another block.

3 For C and D squares, follow directions for Half-Square triangles as provided in Question 147. Make (8) sets.

4 Carefully following the illustration for orientation, sew (4) CD units together. Repeat once more. Press seams in one direction.

5 Sew 4 CD unit to one side of AB. Repeat on opposite side of AB. Press seams.

6 Carefully following the illustration for orientation, sew (5) CD units together. Repeat once more. Press seams in one direction.

7 Sew 5 CD unit to side of AB. Repeat on opposite side of AB. Press seams.

PATCH	No	6"	9"	12"	15"	
A*	1	4 1/2"	6 1/4"	3 1/4"	9 7/8"	■
B*	1	4 1/2"	6 1/4"	3 1/4"	9 7/8"	■
C	8	2"	2 5/8"	8"	3 7/8"	■
D	8	2"	2 5/8"	8"	3 7/8"	■

*There will be an extra triangles from these squares when cut from a triangle.

Question 51:
What is a Monkey Wrench block?

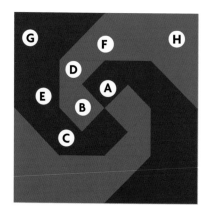

With its interlocking squares and triangles, this block looks just like the tool it's named after. If you're making a masculine-style quilt, consider including this block in the design.

HOW IT'S DONE

1 Cut the patches as shown based on the desired finished block size.

2 Following directions for Four-Patch blocks provided in Question 145 in Chapter 11, make AB center Four-Patch square.

3 With each successive square cut into four triangles and added to the outside of the growing block, follow directions for Square in a Square block as provided in Question 152 in Chapter 11.

PATCH	No	6"	9"	12"	15"
A	2	1 1/2"	2 1/8"	2 5/8"	3 1/8"
B	2	1 1/2"	2 1/8"	2 5/8"	3 1/8"
C	1	2 3/8"	3 1/8"	3 7/8"	4 5/8"
D	1	2 3/8"	3 1/8"	3 7/8"	4 5/8"
E*	1	4 1/4"	5 3/4"	7 1/4"	8 3/4"
F*	1	4 1/4"	5 3/4"	7 1/4"	8 3/4"
G	1	3 7/8"	5 3/8"	6 7/8"	8 3/8"
H	1	3 7/8"	5 3/8"	6 7/8"	8 3/8"

*There will be 2 extra triangles when these squares are cut.

Question 52:
What is a Snail's Trail block?

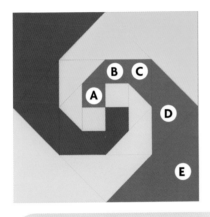

Similar to the Monkey Wrench block, the Snail's Trail adds another swirl with triangles and works with four colors instead of two. You can choose to work with two colors instead.

HOW IT'S DONE

1 Cut the patches as shown above based on the desired finished block size.

2 Following directions for Four-Patch blocks provided in Question 145 in Chapter 11, make AB center Four-Patch square.

3 Cut C and E patches in half diagonally once, corner to corner. Makes (2) triangles of each color patch. You'll only need one of each. Save the remaining for a second block.

4 Cut B and D patches in half twice along the diagonal, corners to corners, forming an X cut. Makes (4) triangles of each color patch. You'll only need (1) of each.

5 Carefully following illustration for correct color placement, sew long edge of B triangles to each side of A Four-Square patch. Press seams toward B.

6 Continue, adding C, D and E to the AB patch. Carefully following illustration for correct color placement, sew long edge of C triangles to each side of AB patch. Press seams toward C.

7 Carefully following illustration for correct color placement, sew long edge of D triangles to each side of ABC patch. Press seams toward D.

8 Carefully following illustration for correct color placement, sew long edge of E triangles to each side of ABCD patch. Press seams toward E.

PATCH	No	6"	9"	12"	15"
A	1**	1 1/4"	1 5/8"	2"	2 3/8"
B*	1**	2 3/4"	3 1/2"	4 1/4"	5"
C	1**	2 3/8"	3 1/8"	3 7/8"	4 5/8"
D*	1**	4 1/4"	5 3/4"	7 1/4"	8 3/4"
E	1**	3 7/8"	5 3/8"	6 7/8"	8 3/8"

* There will be 2 extra triangles when these are cut **1 ea. color, 4 total

Question 53:
What is a Virginia Reel block?

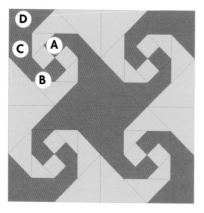

HOW IT'S DONE

1 Cut the patches as shown based on the desired finished block size.

2 Follow the directions in Question 51 to make (4) Monkey Wrench blocks.

3 Following the illustration for placement, arrange four Monkey Wrench blocks in a Four-Patch arrangement. Sew top rows, then bottom row and then row together.

This is a variation on the Monkey Wrench block and consists of four units, two of which are rotated 90 degrees.

PATCH	No	6"	9"	12"	15"
A	4*	1"	1 1/4"	1 1/2"	1 7/8"
B	4*	1 5/8"	2"	2 3/8"	2 3/4"
C	2**	2 3/4"	3 1/2"	4 1/4"	5"
D	4*	2 3/8"	3 1/8"	3 7/8"	4 5/8"

*4 ea. color, 8 total ** 2 ea. color, 8 total

Question 54:
What is a House block?

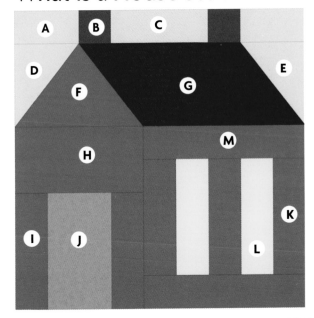

There are many variations of the House block, some of which look like churches, barns, or schoolhouses. This is an example of a simple House block. Consider "fussy cutting" (cutting out a specific element in a printed fabric) some fun-fabric images for the windows or doors.

HOW IT'S DONE

1 Cut the patches as shown above based on the desired block size.

2 To piece the House block, work in rows and sections and carefully follow the illustration for correct placement and orientation of patches.

3 For the top row (chimney), sew A/B/C/B/A in that order. Press seams in one direction.

4 For second row (roof), sew D/F/G/E in that order. Press seams in one direction.

5 For door section, sew long side I to long side of J. Press toward I. Repeat for other side of J. Then sew H to top of IJI unit. Press toward H.

6 For window section, sew K/L/K/L/K in that order. Press seams in one direction. Then sew M patches to top and bottom on KLKLK unit. Press toward Ms.

7 Sew door section to window section. Press seam toward door.

8 Sew 3 rows together. Press seams in one direction.

PATCH	No	6"	9"	12"	15"
A	2	1 1/8" X 1 7/8"	1 1/2" X 2 1/2"	1 7/8" X 3 1/8"	2 1/8" X 3 7/8"
B	2	1 1/8"	1 1/2"	1 7/8"	2 1/8"
C	1	1 1/8" X 2 1/2"	1 1/2" X 3 1/2"	1 7/8" X 4 1/2"	2 1/8" X 5 1/2"
D	1	2 1/8" X 2 5/8"	2 3/4" X 3 1/2"	3 3/8" X 4 1/4"	4 1/8" X 5 1/8"
E*	1	2 1/8" X 2 5/8"	2 3/4" X 3 1/2"	3 3/8" X 4 1/4"	4 1/8" X 5 1/8"
F**	1	2 3/8" X 3 3/4"	3 1/8" X 5"	4" X 6 3/8"	4 7/8" X 7 3/4"
G**	1	2 1/8" X 4"	3" X 5 5/8"	3 7/8" X 7 1/4"	4 5/8" X 9"
H	1	1 7/8" X 3 1/8"	2 1/2" X 4"	3 1/8" X 5 7/8"	3 7/8" X 7 1/8"
I	2	1 1/8" X 2 7/8"	1 1/2" X 4"	1 7/8" X 5 1/8"	2 1/8" X 6 3/8"
J	1	1 7/8" X 2 7/8"	2 1/2" X 4"	3 1/8" 5 1/8"	3 7/8" X 6 3/8"
K	3	1 1/8" X 2 7/8"	1 1/2" X 4"	1 7/8" X 5 1/8"	2 1/8" X 6 3/8"
L	2	1 1/8" X 2 7/8"	1 1/2" X 4"	1 7/8" X 5 1/8"	2 1/8" X 6 3/8"
M	2	1 1/8" X 3 7/8"	1 1/2" X 5 1/2"	1 7/8" X 7 1/8"	2 1/8" X 8 7/8"

*E is the reverse of D. **F and G are cut from templates; the size of rectangle in the table gives enough fabric for cutting the shapes out.

Question 55:
What is a Delectable Mountains block?

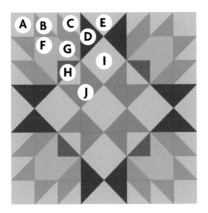

With all of the peaks and valleys created by the placement of Half-Square triangles, the Delectable Mountains block is reminiscent of a mountain range, much like the ones the pioneer women traveled over and through in the early days of American expansion.

HOW IT'S DONE

1 Cut the patches as shown above based on the desired block size.

2 With B and C squares, follow directions for Half-Square triangles as provided in Question 147 in Chapter 11. Make (8) sets.

3 With B and G squares, follow directions for Half-Square triangles as provided in Question 147 in Chapter 11. Make (4) sets.

4 With B and H squares, follow directions for Half-Square triangles as provided in Question 147 in Chapter 11. Make (2) sets.

5 With square D and rectangle E, follow directions for Flying Geese blocks as provided in Question 146 in Chapter 11. Make (4) Flying Geese units.

6 Cut remaining (4) D patches in half diagonally from corner to corner to make (8) D triangles.

7 Cut (6) J patches in half diagonally from corner to corner to make (8) J triangles.

8 Sew (2) D triangles to (2) adjacent sides of square I. Press seams out. Sew (2) J triangles to remaining (2) sides of square I. Press seams out. Repeat (3) more times.

9 Sew J triangles to each side of square I. Press seams out.

10 Carefully following illustration for color placement and patch/unit orientation, assemble units and patches into rows. Sew rows into blocks.

PATCH	No	6"	9"	12"	15"
A	4	1¼"	1⅝"	2"	2⅜"
B	12	1⅝"	2"	2⅜"	2¾"
C	10	1⅝"	2"	2⅜"	2¾"
D	12	1⅝"	2"	2⅜"	2¾"
E	4	1¼" X 2½"	1⅝" X 3¼"	2" X 4"	2⅜" X 4¾"
F	4	1¼"	1⅝"	2"	2⅜"
G	4	1⅝"	2"	2⅜"	2¾"
H	2	1⅝"	2"	2⅜"	2¾"
I	5	1½"	3½"	4¼"	5"
J	6	1⅝"	2"	2⅜"	2¾"

Question 56:
What is a Bridal Path block?

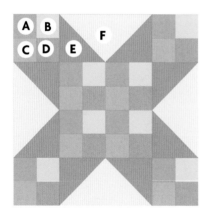

This block is a Sawtooth Star with a chain running through it to reflect the path to becoming a bride, the star of any wedding.

PATCH	No	6"	9"	12"	15"
A	8	1 1/4"	1 5/8"	2"	2 3/8"
B	8	1 1/4"	1 5/8"	2"	2 3/8"
C	8	1 1/4"	1 5/8"	2"	2 3/8"
D	8	1 1/4"	1 5/8"	2"	2 3/8"
E	8	2"	2 7/8"	3 1/2"	4 1/8"
F	4	2" X 4"	3 1/8" X 5 1/4"	3 1/2" X 6 1/2"	4 1/8" X 8 1/4"

HOW IT'S DONE

1 Cut the patches as shown above based on the desired finished block size.

2 With A, B, C, and D squares, follow directions for Four-Patch blocks as provided in Question 145 in Chapter 11. Make (8) Four-Patch units.

3 For the center patch, carefully follow illustration for correct placement and sew (4) Four-Patch units together, top row, bottom row and row together. Press seams.

4 With square E and rectangle F, follow directions for Flying Geese blocks as provided in Question 146 in Chapter 11. Make (4) Flying Geese units.

5 Following illustration for correct placement, sew one Four-Patch to the short edge of Flying Geese unit. Press to Flying Geese unit. Repeat on opposite side of Flying Geese unit.

6 Repeat Step 5 once more. Set aside.

7 Sew Flying Geese unit to edge of center Four Patch unit. Press seam to Flying Geese unit. Repeat on opposite side of center Four Patch unit.

8 Sew rows together. Press seams in one direction.

Question 57:
What is a Dutch Rose block?

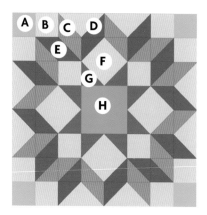

This block is also known as the Carpenter's Wheel. Its three-dimensional appearance comes from the shading of the diamonds surrounding the center Sawtooth Star. This version is made with triangles instead of diamonds so there are no Y-seams to wrestle with, making it suitable for beginners.

PATCH	No	6"	9"	12"	15"
A	4	1 1/4"	1 5/8"	2"	2 3/8"
B	12	1 1/4"	1 5/8"	2"	2 3/8"
C	14	1 5/8"	2"	2 3/8"	2 3/4"
D	8	1 5/8"	3 1/2"	4 1/4"	5"
E	14	1 5/8"	2"	2 3/8"	2 3/4"
F	4	1 1/2"	2 1/8"	2 5/8"	3 1/8"
G	4	1 5/8"	2"	2 3/8"	2 3/4"
H	1	2"	2 3/4"	3 1/2"	4 1/4"

HOW IT'S DONE

1 Cut the patches as shown based on the desired block size.

2 Cut (2) C patches, (2) E patches, and (4) G patches in half diagonally from corner to corner, making (4) triangles of C, (4) triangles of E, and (8) triangles of G.

3 Sew E triangle to one side of F square. Press seam out. Sew C triangle to adjacent right side of F square. Press seam out. Sew (2) G triangles to remaining (2) sides of F square. Press seams out. Repeat (3) more times.

4 Layer (1) square C with (1) square E, right sides together with the lighter square on top. Draw a diagonal line on top square from corner to corner.

5 Sew a ¼ inch seam along each side of drawn line.

6 Cut along drawn line (makes two Half-Square triangle units) and press each unit's seam toward darker patch.

7 Repeat (5) more times with C and E patches. You'll have (12) Half-Square CE units when done.

8 Carefully following illustration for correct color placement and unit orientation, sew Four-Patch unit with (3) CE Half-Square units and (1) B patch. Repeat (3) more times.

9 Sew rows for inside unit as follows:
- Row 1: CE/B Four-Patch, CEGF unit, CE/B Four-Patch
- Row 2: CEFG unit, H patch, CEFG unit
- Row 3: CE/B Four-Patch, CEGF unit, CE/B Four-Patch

10 Sew rows together.

11 From (4) D patches and (4) E patches, make (8) Half-Square triangle units.

12 From (4) D patches and (4) C patches, make (8) Half-Square triangle units.

13 Carefully following illustration for correct color placement and unit orientation, sew border units of A patches, B patches, CD and ED units to inner unit. Press seams.

58 What is a Log Cabin block?

59 What is a Courthouse Steps block?

60 What is a Pineapple block?

61 What is an Ocean Waves block?

62 What is a Shadows block?

63 What is an Irish Chain block?

64 What is a LeMoyne Star?

65 What is a Hunter's Star block?

66 What is a Nosegay block?

67 What is a Double Star block?

68 What is a Pine Burr block?

69 What is a Harlequin Star block?

70 What is a Crossroads block?

71 What is a New York Beauty block?

72 What is a Winding Ways block?

73 What is an Attic Windows block?

74 What is a Kaleidoscope block?

75 What is a Fan block?

76 What is a Dresden Plate block?

77 What is an alternate Dresden Plate block with rounded blades?

78 What is a Double Wedding Ring quilt?

79 What is a Grandmother's Flower Garden quilt?

80 What is a Thousand Pyramids quilt?

81 What is a Trip Around the World quilt?

82 What is a Lone Star quilt?

83 What is a Tumbling Blocks quilt?

84 What is a Mariner's Compass quilt?

NO-GRID BLOCKS
AND QUILTS

Question 58:
What is a Log Cabin block?

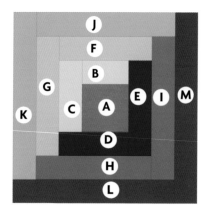

HOW IT'S DONE

1 Cut the patches as shown based on the desired finished block size.

2 After adding each strip, press seams toward outside edge of block.

3 Sew strip B to square A.

4 Sew strip C to AB unit.

5 Continue sewing strips in order, carefully following illustration for correct color placement.

This block is built from rectangular "logs" of fabric sewn around a center square. The Log Cabin gets its name from the way the block is constructed with one round of strips building upon the previous, just as the walls of a log cabin were built.

PATCH	NO	6"	9"	12"	15"
A	1	2"	2 ¾"	3 ½"	4 ¼"
B	1	1 ¼" X 2"	1 ⅝" X 2 ¾"	2" X 3 ½"	2 ⅜" X 4 ¼"
C	1	1 ¼" X 2 ¾"	1 ⅝" X 3 ⅞"	2" X 5"	2 ⅜" X 6 ⅛"
D	1	1 ¼" X 2 ¾"	1 ⅝" X 3 ⅞"	2" X 5"	2 ⅜" X 6 ⅛"
E	1	1 ¼" X 3 ½"	1 ⅝" X 5"	2" X 6 ½"	2 ⅜" X 8"
F	1	1 ¼" X 3 ½"	1 ⅝" X 5"	2" X 6 ½"	2 ⅜" X 8"
G	1	1 ¼" X 4 ¼"	1 ⅝" X 6 ⅛"	2" X 8"	2 ⅜" X 9 ⅞"
H	1	1 ¼" X 4 ½"	1 ⅝" X 6 ⅛"	2" X 8"	2 ⅜" X 9 ⅞"
I	1	1 ¼" X 5"	1 ⅝" X 7 ¼"	2" X 9 ½"	2 ⅜" X 11 ¾"
J	1	1 ¼" X 5"	1 ⅝" X 7 ¼"	2" X 9 ½"	2 ⅜" X 11 ¾"
K	1	1 ¼" X 5 ¾"	1 ⅝" X 8 ⅜"	2" X 11"	2 ⅜" X 13 ⅝"
L	1	1 ¼" X 5 ¾"	1 ⅝" X 8 ⅜"	2" X 11"	2 ⅜" X 13 ⅝"
M	1	1 ¼" X 6 ½"	1 ⅝" X 9 ½"	2" X 12 ½"	2 ⅜" X 15 ½"

Question 59:
What is a Courthouse Steps block?

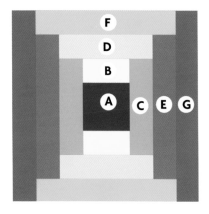

This is a variation of the Log Cabin block, but instead of the strips being added around the center square, they are sewn to opposite sides of the center square giving the appearance of a flight of steps.

HOW IT'S DONE

1 Cut the patches as shown based on the desired finished block size.

2 After adding each strip, press seams toward outside edge of block.

3 Sew strips B to opposite sides square A.

4 Sew strips C to opposite sides of AB unit.

5 Continue sewing strips in this manner, carefully following illustration for correct color placement.

PATCH	No	6"	9"	12"	15"	
A	1	2"	2 ¾"	3 ½"	4 ¼"	☐
B	2	1 ¼" X 2"	1 ⅝" X 2 ¾"	2" X 3 ½"	2 ⅜" 4 ¼"	▬
C	2	1 ¼" X 3 ½"	1 ⅝" X 5"	2" X 6 ½"	2 ⅜" X 8"	▬
D	2	1 ¼" X 3 ½"	1 ⅝" X 5"	2" X 6 ½"	2 ⅜" X 8"	▬
E	2	1 ¼" X 5"	1 ⅝" X 7 ¼"	2" X 9 ½"	2 ⅜" X 11 ¾"	▬
F	2	1 ¼" X 5"	1 ⅝" X 7 ¼"	2" X 9 ½"	2 ⅜" X 11 ¾"	▬
G	2	1 ¼" X 6 ½"	1 ⅝" X 9 ½"	2" X 12 ½"	2 ⅜" X 15 ½"	▬

Question 60:
What is a Pineapple block?

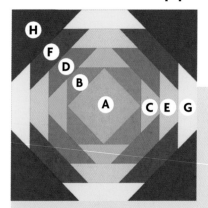

Yet another variation of the Log Cabin block, this version features triangles in the corners, making the block resemble a pineapple.

You've created a Square in a Square.

3 Line up rectangle C to one side of AB square right sides together and sew. Press seam to rectangle and repeat in turn with 3 remaining rectangle Cs.

4 Take triangle D and with the point facing into the ABC block and right sides together, position it in ABC's corner. Sew a ¼ inch seam along the long edge of triangle D and then press triangle open to the outside corner. Repeat with 3 remaining triangle Ds.

HOW IT'S DONE

1 Cut the patches as shown based on the desired finished block size. Square patch A stays whole. Square patches B, D, F, and H are cut in half on the diagonal, making 2 triangles from each. Rectangles C, E, and G stay whole.

2 Starting with A and one triangle B, line up long outside edges, right sides together and sew. Press seam to triangle and repeat 3 remaining triangle Bs.

5 Line up rectangle E to one side of ABCD square right sides together and sew. Press seam to rectangle and repeat in turn with 3 remaining rectangle Es.

6 Repeat for the remaining triangles and rectangles, building the Pineapple block one piece at a time until done.

PATCH	No	6"	9"	12"	15"
A	1	2 ¼"	3"	3 ⅞"	4 ¾"
B	2	2 ⅜"	3"	3 ⅝"	4 ¼"
C	4	1 ⅛" X 2 ⅜"	1 ⅜" X 3 ¾"	1 ¾" X 4 ⅝"	2" X 5 ½"
D	2	2 ½"	3 ¼"	4"	4 ⅞"
E	4	1 ⅛" X 3 ⅜"	1 ⅜" X 4 ½"	1 ¾" X 5 ⅝"	2" X 6 ¾"
F	2	2 ¾"	3 ¾"	4 ¾"	5 ¾"
G	4	1 ⅛" X 3 ⅞"	1 ⅜" X 5 ¼"	1 ¾" X 6 ⅝"	2" X 5 ½"
H	2	3 ⅛"	4 ¼"	5 ⅜"	6 ½"

Question 61:
What is an Ocean Waves block?

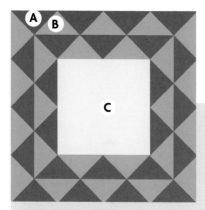

With its many triangles, the Ocean Waves block resembles ripples on the ocean. It is usually sewn in blues, greens, and lavenders to reflect the colors of water.

HOW IT'S DONE

1 Cut the patches as shown above based on the desired finished block size.

2 The block will be constructed in the Square in a Square manner, starting with four triangle units sewn to each edge of the center patch.

3 Cut A and B patches in half twice, along the diagonal corners to corners, forming an X cut. Makes (24) triangles of each color patch.

4 For the 4-triangle unit A, sew A, B, A along short sides in a row. B is inverted. Press seams to As. Sew A triangle to B along long edges of both triangles. Press toward A. Repeat (5) times more.

5 Sew long edge of (1) 4-triangle unit A to edge of center patch C. Press toward C. Repeat on opposite side.

6 For the 4-triangle unit B, sew B, A, B along short sides in a row. A is inverted. Press seams toward As. Sew B triangle to A along long edges of both triangles. Press toward B. Repeat (5) times.

7 Sew long edge of (1) 4-triangle unit B to edge of center patch C. Press toward C. Repeat on opposite side.

8 For 8-triangle units, carefully follow illustration for color placement. Sew (1) triangle unit A to (1) triangle unit B along short side. Press. Altogether, make (2) 8-triangle units with A unit on right side and (2) 8-triangle units with A on left side.

9 Following illustration for placement, sew 8-triangle unit to long edge of triangle/center patch unit. Press seam out. Repeat on remaining three sides.

PATCH	No	6"	9"	12"	15"
A	6	2 ¾"	3 ½"	4 ¼"	5"
B	6	2 ¾"	3 ½"	4 ¼"	5"
C	1	3 ½"	5"	6 ½"	7 ½"

Question 62:
What is a Shadows block?

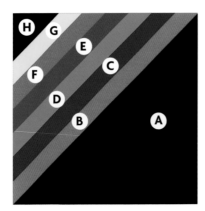

This block is sometimes made from scraps or "strings" of fabric left over from other projects. Because these fabrics may not be cut on the straight grain, a foundation of paper or muslin is sometimes used as a stabilizer. When the large triangle of fabric in the corner is a darker color, it looks like it's casting a shadow.

HOW IT'S DONE

1 Cut the patches as shown based on the desired finished block size.

2 Cut the A and H squares in half diagonally from corner to corner.

3 Sew B to A, then C to B and continue sewing strips in alphabetical order.

4 Trim block to its correct finished size (6 ½", 9 ½", 12 ½", or 15 ½") using a square rotary ruler. Use the 45-degree angle on the ruler to line up the center diagonal of the block. Press seams toward A triangle.

PATCH	No	6"	9"	12"	15"
A	1	6 7/8"	9 7/8"	12 7/8"	15 7/8" X 5 ½"
B	1	1" X 9 ¾"	1 ¼" X 13 7/8"	1 5/8" X 18 1/8"	1 ¾" X 22 3/8"
C	1	1" X 8 5/8"	1 3/8" X 12 3/8"	1 5/8" X 16 1/8"	1 7/8" X 19 ¾"
D	1	1" X 7 5/8"	1 ¼" X 10 ¾"	1 5/8" X 13 7/8"	1 7/8" X 17 1/8"
E	1	1" X 6 ½"	1 ¼" X 9 1/8"	1 ½" X 11 ¾"	1 7/8" X 14 ½"
F	1	1" X 5 ½"	1 ¼" X 7 5/8"	1 5/8" X 9 5/8"	1 7/8" X 11 ¾"
G	1	1"X 4 3/8"	1 ¼" X 6"	1 ½" X 7 ½"	1 7/8" X 9 1/8"
H	1	2 3/8"	3 1/8"	3 7/8"	4 5/8"

Question 63:
What is an Irish Chain block?

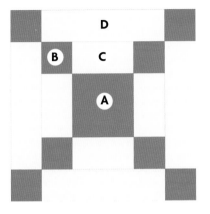

The Irish Chain block is an excellent way to join different types of blocks together with an alternating block. It gets its name from the chain linking the blocks along the diagonal.

Piecing is similar to the Log Cabin block, with the patches added to the center square. This block can be strip pieced.

HOW IT'S DONE

1 Cut the patches as shown based on the desired finished block size.

2 Sew (2) B squares to end of C strip. Press seams to C. Repeat one more time.

3 Sew C strip's long edge to A square. Press seam to C. Repeat on opposite side.

4 Sew BC unit to long edge of A CAC unit. Press to BC. Repeat on opposite side.

5 Sew (2) B squares to end of D strip. Press seams to D. Repeat one more time.

6 Sew D strip's long edge to ABC square. Press seam to D. Repeat on opposite side.

7 Sew BD unit to long edge of ABC unit. Press to D. Repeat on opposite side.

PATCH	No	6"	9"	12"	15"
A	1	2 ½"	3 ½"	4 ½"	5 ½"
B	8	1 ½"	2"	2 ½"	3"
C	4	1 ½" X 2 ½"	2" X 3 ½"	2 ½" X 4 ½"	3" X 5 ½"
D	4	1 ½" X 4 ½"	2" X 6 ½"	2 ½" X 8 ½"	3" X 10 ½"

Question 64:
What is a LeMoyne Star?

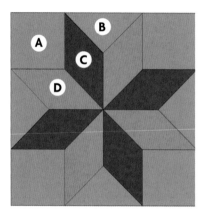

The LeMoyne Star is the most basic of the eight-pointed stars. Formed with diamonds, it is considered the grandmother of the Lone Star quilt. Its construction includes inset Y-seams, which makes it a bit more challenging. Refer to Question 150 on page 167 for instructions on Y-seams.

HOW IT'S DONE

1 Cut the patches as shown based on the desired finished block size.

2 Sew (1) C diamond to (1) D diamond so C diamond is on the right side when opened facing right side up. Repeat (3) more times. Press seams towards darker fabric.

3 Sew (2) CD units together to make half the star. Repeat. Press seams towards dark diamond.

4 Sew halves together to make star. Press seam.

5 Sew A to CD unit using Y-seam construction method. Repeat (3) more times.

6 Sew E triangles to remaining CD areas using Y-seam constructions method. Press.

PATCH	No.	6"	9"	12"	15"
A	4	2 ¼"	3 ⅛"	4"	4 ⅞"
B	1	4"	5"	6 ¼"	7 ½"
C	4	1 ¾" X 2 ½"	2 ⅜" X 3 ⅜"	3" X 4 ¼"	3 ⅝" X 5 ⅛"
D	4	1 ¾" X 2 ½"	2 ⅜" X 3 ⅜"	3" X 4 ¼"	3 ⅝" X 5 ⅛"

Question 65:
What is a Hunter's Star block?

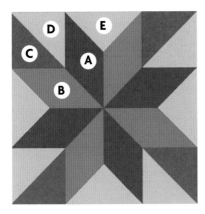

This variation on a LeMoyne Star creates a secondary pattern at the block intersections.

HOW IT'S DONE

1 Cut the patches as shown based on the desired finished block size.

2 With C and D square, follow directions for Half-Square triangles as provided in Question 147 in Chapter 11. Make (2) sets.

3 Sew (1) A diamond to (1) B diamond so A diamond is on the right side when opened facing right side up. Repeat (3) more times. Press seams to darker fabric.

4 Sew CD to AB unit using Y-seam construction method. Repeat (3) more times.

5 Sew E triangles to remaining AB areas using Y-seam construction method. Press.

PATCH	No	6"	9"	12"	15"	
A	4	1 ¾" X 2 ½"	2 ³/8" X 3 ³/8"	3" X 4 ¼"	3 ⁵/8" X 5 ⁵/8"	
B	4	1 ¾" X 2 ½"	2 ³/8" X 3 ³/8"	3" X 4 ¼"	3 ⁵/8" X 5 ⁵/8"	
C	2	2 ⁵/8"	3 ½"	4 ³/8"	5 ¼"	
D	2	2 ⁵/8"	3 ½"	4 ³/8"	5 ¼"	
E	1	3 ¾"	5"	6 ¼"	7 ½"	

Question 66:
What is a Nosegay block?

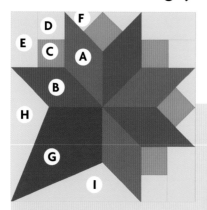

A Nosegay block is a variation of the Lemoyne Star, but is cleverly adapted to look like a bouquet of flowers, making a Nosegay quilt a wonderful wedding gift.

HOW IT'S DONE

1 Cut the patches as shown based on the desired finished block size. Cut pieces A and B from templates.

2 Sew (1) A diamond to (1) B diamond so A diamond is on the right side when opened facing right side up. Repeat twice. Press seams toward darker fabric.

3 Sew C to D. Press seam toward darker fabric. Sew E to CD. Press seam toward E. Repeat (2) more times.

4 Cut F in half diagonally from corner to corner. Repeat to create (4) triangles.

5 Sew short side of F to C, carefully following illustration. Repeat on other side of C. Press seams toward F. Repeat once more on last C block.

6 Sew CDE to AB unit using Y-seam construction method. Repeat twice. Sew ABCDE units together.

7 Sew H and I to opposite long sides of G. Sew GHI unit to corner of ABCDE unit.

8 Sew FCF units to remaining AB areas using Y-seam constructions method. Press.

PATCH	No	6"	9"	12"	15"	
A	1	1 ¾" X 2 ½"	2 ⅜" X 3 ⅜"	3" X 4 ¼"	3 ⅝" X 5 ⅛"	
B	1	1 ¾" X 2 ½"	2 ⅜" X 3 ⅜"	3" X 4 ¼"	3 ⅝" X 5 ⅛"	
C	2	1 ⅜"	1 ¾"	2 ¼"	2 ¾"	
D	2	1 ⅜"	1 ¾"	2 ¼"	2 ¾"	
E	2	1 ⅜" X 2 ¼"	1 ¾" X 3 ⅛"	2 ¼" X 4"	2 ¾" X 4 ½"	
F	2	2 ½"	3 ⅛"	3 ¾"	4 ⅜"	
G	1	3 ½"	5"	6 ½"	8"	
H*	1	1 ¾" X 6 ⅛"	2 ⅜" X 8 ¼"	3" X 10 ⅜"	3 ⅝" X 12 ½"	
I*	1	1 ¾" X 6 ⅛"	2 ⅜" X 8 ¼"	3" X 10 ⅜"	3 ⅝" X 12 ½"	

*Patches H and I are mirror images of each other. A, B, and G are cut from templates.

Question 67:
What is a Double Star block?

Sometimes called a Rising Star block, the Double Star is a smaller Variable Star set inside a larger Variable Star. Start by constructing the inside star and add the elements for the outside star.

HOW IT'S DONE

1 Cut the patches as shown above based on the desired finished block size.

2 For inside star, use square C and rectangle B and follow directions for Flying Geese blocks as provided in Question 146 in Chapter 11. Make (4) BC Flying Geese units.

3 Arrange the patches as shown above for the inside star. Sew rows as follows:
• Row 1: D, BC, D
• Row 2: BC, A, BC
• Row 3: D, BC, D

4 Sew Row 2 to Row 1. Sew Row 3 to Row 2. Press seams to inside star's outer edges.

5 For inside star, use square F and rectangle E and follow directions for Flying Geese blocks as provided in Question 146 in Chapter 11. Make (4) EF Flying Geese units.

6 Sew Flying Geese EF to top of inside star. Repeat on bottom of inside star. Press seams out.

7 Sew (1) patch G to either side of Flying Geese unit EF following illustration for placement. Press seams to G. Repeat on last Flying Geese unit EF.

8 Sew EFG units to either side of inner star. Press seams to outer edge.

PATCH	No	6"	9"	12"	15"
A	1	2"	2 ¾"	3 ½"	4 ¼"
B	4	1 ¼" X 2"	1 ⅝" X 2 ¾"	2" X 3 ½"	2 ⅜" X 4 ¼"
C	8	1 ¼"	1 ⅝"	2"	2 ⅜"
D	4	1 ¼"	1 ⅝"	2"	2 ⅜"
E	4	2" X 3 ½"	2 ¾" X 5"	3 ½" X 6 ½"	4 ¼" X 8"
F	8	2"	2 ¾"	3 ½"	4 ¼"
G	4	2"	2 ¾"	3 ½"	4 ¼"

Question 68:
What is a Pine Burr block?

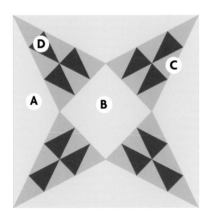

This block looks like a pine cone with its many triangles radiating out from the center. It's a visually striking block with the potential to really jazz up a quilt's design.

HOW IT'S DONE

1 Following the chart for the finished size block desired, cut triangles A, C and D using templates found on pages 218-219.

2 Following the block's illustration, sew 6 C and 3 D triangles to create larger pieced triangles. Repeat 3 times.

3 Sew CD triangle's base to side B patch. Repeat 3 times.

4 Following directions on page 167 for sewing Y-seams, sew 1 A between each CD triangle wedge. Repeat 3 times. Press seams.

PATCH	No.	9"	12"	15"	18"	
A*	4	2 ¾" X 11 ⅛"	3 ½" X 14 ⅛"	4 ¼" X 17 ⅛"	5" X 20 ⅛"	▲
B	1	3 ⅝"	4 ¾"	5 ¾"	6 ⅞"	■
C*	24	2 ⅝" X 1 ¾"	3 ⅛" X 2 ⅛"	3 ¾" X 2 ½"	4 ¼" X 2 ⅞"	▲
D*	12	2 ⅝" X 1 ¾"	3 ⅛" X 2 ⅛"	3 ¾" X 2 ½"	4 ¼" X 2 ⅞"	▲

*The dimensions given for patches A, C, and D are for isosceles triangles. Cut the strips in the first measurement given. The triangles' bases will be cut from the second measurement. The angles of each triangle are provided on the templates on page 218.

Question 69:
What is a Harlequin Star block?

This block is similar to the Pine Burr block but has a slightly different coloration, with the points usually the same color as the center square.

HOW IT'S DONE

1 Following the chart for the finished size block desired, cut triangles A, C, and D using templates found on pages 218-219.

2 Piece the C, D and E patches to create the larger triangle wedge. Repeat (3) more times.

3 Sew triangle wedge to side of patch B. Press seam toward B. Repeat (3) more times to complete patch B.

4 Following directions page 167 for sewing Y-seams on, sew 1 A between each CDE triangle wedge. Repeat 3 times. Press seams.

PATCH	No.	9"	12"	15"	18"	
A*	4	2 ¾" X 11 ⅛"	3 ½" X 14 ⅛"	4 ¼" X 17 ⅛"	5" X 20 ⅛"	▲
B	1	3 ⅝"	4 ¾"	5 ¾"	6 ⅞"	■
C*	4	2 ⅝" X 1 ¾"	3 ⅛" X 2 ⅛"	3 ¾" X 2 ½"	4 ¼" X 2 ⅞"	▲
D*	12	2 ⅝" X 1 ¾"	3 ⅛" X 2 ⅛"	3 ¾" X 2 ½"	4 ¼" X 2 ⅞"	▲
E*	20	2 ⅝" X 1 ¾"	3 ⅛" X 2 ⅛"	3 ¾" X 2 ½"	4 ¼" X 2 ⅞"	▲

*The dimensions given for patches A, C, D, and E are for isosceles triangles. They are first cut from strips.

Question 70:
What is a Crossroads block?

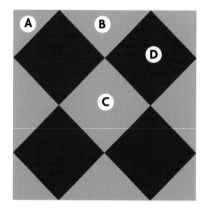

Simple squares on point give the Crossroad block an interesting perspective, resembling floor tiles. The block is pieced on the diagonal with the corner triangles added last.

HOW IT'S DONE

1 Cut the patches as shown above based on the desired finished block size.

2 Cut A patches in half on diagonal corner to corner. Makes (4) triangles.

3 Cut B patch in half twice, along the diagonal corner to corner, forming an X cut. Makes (4) triangles.

4 Assemble patches on point and sew rows as follows, alternating seams from row to row:

- Row 1: A
- Row 2: B, D, B
- Row 3: A, D, C, D, A
- Row 4: B, D, B
- Row 5: A

5 Sew rows together. Press seams in one direction.

PATCH	No	6"	9"	12"	15"
A	2	2 ³⁄₈"	3 ¹⁄₈"	3 ⁷⁄₈"	4 ⁵⁄₈"
B	1	4 ¼"	5 ¾"	7 ¼"	8 ¾"
C	1	2 ⁵⁄₈"	3 ⁵⁄₈"	4 ¾"	5 ¾"
D	4	2 ⁵⁄₈"	3 ⁵⁄₈"	4 ¾"	5 ¾"

Question 71:
What is a New York Beauty block?

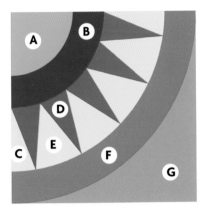

This block gets its name from its resemblance to the crown on the Statue of Liberty. When several blocks are joined together, they look like a rising sun or a series of fans. It makes a gorgeous quilt when repeated in an overall quilt design.

HOW IT'S DONE

1 Following the chart for the finished size block desired, cut patches for all pieces.

2 Sew crown in this order: C, D, E, D, E, D, E, D, E, D, C.

3 Following directions page 157 for piecing curves on, sew B to A matching centers and ends.

4 Sew crown to B matching centers and ends.

5 Sew F to crown matching centers and ends.

6 Sew corner G to F matching centers and ends. Press seams.

PATCH	No	6"	9"	12"	15"	
A	1	2 ½"	3 ½"	4 ½"	5 ½"	●
B	1	3 ½"	5"	6 ½"	8"	●
C	2	1 ½" X 3 ½"	2" X 5"	3" X 6 ½"	4" X 8"	■
D	5	1 ½" X 3 ½"	2" X 5"	3" X 6 ½"	4" X 8"	■
E	4	1 ½" X 3 ½"	2" X 5"	3" X 6 ½"	4" X 8"	■
F	1	6 ½"	9 ½"	12 ½"	15 ½"	●
G	1	6 ½"	9 ½"	12 ½"	15 ½"	■

This block can be made by templates as a paper-pieced block. Either way, the patches can be precut from the sizes indicated in the table above.

Question 72:
What is a Winding Ways block?

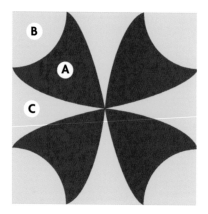

The Winding Ways block looks like a four-leaf clover, but when set with others, it creates a wheel image.

HOW IT'S DONE

1 Following the chart for the finished size block desired, cut patches for A, B and C using templates found on page 223.

2 Following directions on page 157 for piecing curves, sew C to A matching centers and ends. Repeat (3) more times.

3 Sew B to A. Press. Repeat (3) more times.

4 Sew ABC units in pairs. Press seams. Sew pairs together. Press seams.

PATCH	No	6"	9"	12"	15"
A	4	3 ½"	5"	6 ½"	8"
B	4	3"	4"	5"	6"
C	4	3 ½"	5"	6 ½"	8"

Question 73:
What is an Attic Windows block?

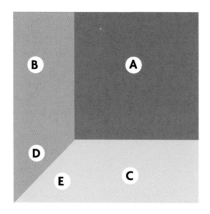

The tones of the fabric used in the Attic Windows block create a three-dimensional effect. It looks like a shadow box or window, which makes a wonderful opportunity to use a landscape or novelty print for patch A. Traditionally this block is constructed with Y-seams, but this simpler version uses a Half-Square triangle instead.

HOW IT'S DONE

1 Cut the patches as shown based on the desired finished block size.

2 For the center Half-Square triangle unit, layer square D with square E, right sides together with the lighter square on top. Draw a diagonal line on top square from corner to corner.

3 Sew a ¼-inch seam along each side of drawn line.

4 Cut along drawn line (makes two Half-Square triangle units) and press each unit's seam toward darker patch. You will only need one Half-Square triangle unit. Save the remaining one for another block.

5 Sew B to A. Press to A.

6 Sew DE to C. Press to C.

7 Sew AB to CDE, press to AB.

PATCH	No	6"	9"	12"	15"	
A	1	4 ½"	6 ½"	8 ½"	10 ½"	■
B	1	2 ½" X 4 ½"	3 ½" X 6 ½"	4 ½" X 8 ½"	5 ½" X 10 ½"	■
C	1	2 ½" X 4 ½"	3 ½" X 6 ½"	4 ½" X 8 ½"	5 ½" X 10 ½"	■
D	1	2 ⅞"	3 ⅞"	4 ⅞"	5 ⅞"	■
E	1	2 ⅞"	3 ⅞"	4 ⅞"	5 ⅞"	■

Question 74:
What is a Kaleidoscope block?

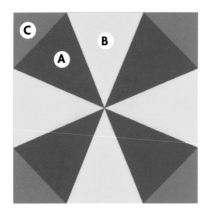

HOW IT'S DONE

1 Following the chart for the finished size block desired, cut wedges for A and B using templates found on page 217. Cut C according to finished block size desired.

2 Sew A and B wedges together in pairs.

3 Sew (2) pairs together to create half of the block. Sew 2 halves together.

4 Sew C triangles to ends of A. Press.

This is the simplest form of this block. It looks like the design you would see when looking through a child's kaleidoscope.

PATCH	No	6"	9"	12"	15"
A	4	4" X 3"	5 ½" X 4 ½"	7" X 8"	5 ½" X 4 ½"
B	4	4" X 3"	5 ½" X 4 ½"	7" X 8"	5 ½" X 4 ½"
C	4	2 ⁵⁄₈"	3 ½"	4 ³⁄₈"	5 ¼"

Question 75:
What is a Fan block?

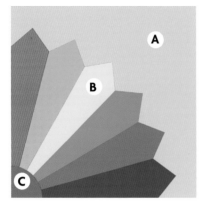

A Fan block is one quarter of a Dresden Plate block. It can be made with rounded or pointed blades. Typically this block is made using a different fabric for each blade. The block uses a combination of appliqué and piecing.

HOW IT'S DONE

1 Following the chart for the finished size block desired, cut wedge for B using templates found on page 215. Cut A and C according to finished block size desired.

2 Fold a triangle over at the blade's wide end to form a point. Tack the end down to hold in place. Repeat for remaining blades.

3 Sew blades together in pairs, then sew pairs together until all 6 blades form fan shape. Press all blade seam allowances to one side.

4 Pin fan to background, then appliqué the blades to background square A, either by hand, using a tiny, close slip stitch along the fan's edge, with thread matching background square A, or by machine, setting the stitch to a narrow zigzag.

5 Cut circle C in half twice, creating (4) quarters. Carefully turn under raw curved edge of C and hand appliqué to corner of fan unit.

PATCH	No	6"	9"	12"	15"	
A	1	6 ½"	9 ½"	12 ½"	15 ½"	■
B	1*	4 ½" X 2"	6 ½" X 3"	8 ½" X 4"	10 ½" X 5"	▬
C**	1	2 ½"	3 ½"	4 ½"	5 ½"	●

*1 each color blade, 6 total. **C is a template.

Question 76:
What is a Dresden Plate block?

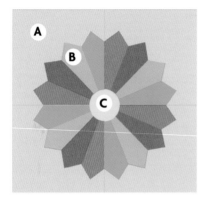

A Dresden Plate block is a pieced circular block or plate made with many different fabrics to provide interest. The blades can be pointed or rounded (see alternate block on page 105.)

HOW IT'S DONE

1 Cut the size and number of patches as shown in the chart below. (The blades are cut from a strip of fabric the size below and a template may be used once the strip is cut.)

2 Sew the wide ends of the blade to create the point.

3 Sew the blades together in pairs; sew the pairs together until all 16 blades form the plate shape. Press all blade seam allowances to one side.

4 The blades are appliquéd to square A by hand or machine.

5 Appliqué or stitch as a curved seam quarter circle C to the blades covering all seam allowances of the blades. Press.

PATCH	No	6"	9"	12"	15"
A	1	6 ½"	9 ½"	12 ½"	15 ½"
B	4*	2 ½" X 1 ½"	3" X 2"	4 ½" X 2 ½"	6" X 3"
C	1	2"	3"	4"	5"

*each color, 16 in total

Question 77:
What is an alternate Dresden Plate block with rounded blades?

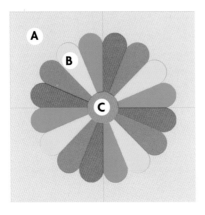

A Fan block is one quarter of a Dresden Plate block. It can be made with rounded or pointed blades. Typically this block is made using a different fabric for each blade. The block uses a combination of appliqué and piecing.

HOW IT'S DONE

1 Cut the size and number of patches as shown in the chart below. (The blades are cut from a strip of fabric the size below and a template may be used once the strip is cut.)

2 Sew the blades together in pairs; sew the pairs together until all 16 blades form the plate shape. Press all blade seam allowances to one side.

3 The blades are appliquéd to square A by hand or machine, as in the previous block.

4 Appliqué or stitch as a curved seam quarter circle C to the blades covering all seam allowances of the blades. Press.

PATCH	No	6"	9"	12"	15"	
A	1	6 ½"	9 ½"	12 ½"	15 ½"	■
B	4*	2 ½" X 1 ½"	3" X 2"	4 ½" X 2 ½"	6" X 3"	▬
C	1	2"	3"	4"	5"	●

*each color, 16 in total

Question 78:
What is a Double Wedding Ring quilt?

The Double Wedding Ring quilt is a traditional quilt made for a bride's hope chest. It consists of interlocking rings and several different fabrics for the rings so the design sparkles. One of the more complicated patchwork quilts to make, Double Wedding Ring quilts feature curved piecing, precisely pieced patches and a scalloped border. Similar patchwork blocks and designs mimic the feel of the Double Wedding Ring quilt but offer easier piecing options.

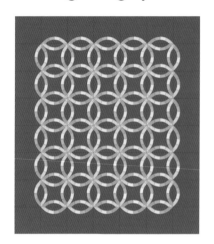

Question 79:
What is a Grandmother's Flower Garden quilt?

Grandmother's Flower Garden quilts are made from hexagons stitched together, usually by hand, to form an overall design. A perfect hand project, most Flower Garden quilts use English paper-piecing techniques for the construction. In English paper-piecing, the patch of fabric is basted to a paper template ranging in size from ½ to 3 inches, depending on the design and size of the finished quilt.

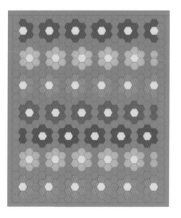

Question 80:
What is a Thousand Pyramids quilt?

This quilt is popular with charm square collectors. An old quilt tradition says that a woman cannot marry until she has collected at least a thousand different fabrics from family and friends for her wedding quilt. The finished quilt was intended to help the young couple as they started their new life by bringing the love and good wishes of all those who donated the charm squares. In the Thousand Pyramids quilt, each triangle is cut from a separate fabric. The diagram shows only one of many possible color arrangements.

Question 81:
What is a Trip Around the World quilt?

Starting with a central square or squares set on-point (see Question 158 for an explanation of the term "on-point"), this quilt's design is created by laying perimeters of the same-sized fabric squares around the center. Each perimeter is made from a different fabric and its squares are also set on-point. This is another pleasing arrangement for using up small scraps of fabric.

Question 82:
What is a Lone Star quilt?

A Lone Star quilt is sometimes called the Bethlehem Star or the Star of Texas and is a large LeMoyne Star with points composed of diamonds. It is a one-block quilt, and space surrounding the star provides a great opportunity for a quilter to show off her beautiful quilting designs.

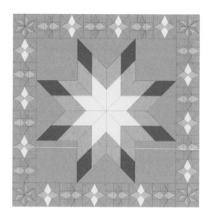

Question 83:
What is a Tumbling Blocks quilt?

This quilt gets its name from a child's toy blocks, and was often used for baby quilts. Careful color placement gives the quilt a three-dimensional effect. It is made from diamonds set together to form interlocking hexagons.

Question 84:
What is a Mariner's Compass quilt?

This quilt gets its name from the compass rose and was traditionally given to people leaving their homes to travel or settle in far-off places. The quilt was also given to seamen and fishermen by their wives to bring them safely back to shore after sailing. It would make a treasured keepsake for anyone embarking on a new chapter in life.

85 What do I need to know to get started with patchwork?

86 I'm just starting. What should my first patchwork quilt be?

87 What tools and materials will I need?

88 Help! I'm trying to set up my work space...

89 Can you tell me what the parts of a patchwork quilt are?

90 What sewing machine should I buy?

91 How do I take care of my sewing machine?

92 What accessories and attachments do I need to make patchwork quilts?

93 Is ironing a big deal in patchwork?

7

PATCHWORK BASICS

Question 85:
What do I need to know to get started with patchwork?

Many patchwork blocks are well suited for beginner quilters because they are made up of fabric units sewn along straight lines (squares, rectangles, and triangles). If you can thread your needle (hand or machine) and sew a straight line, you should be able to accomplish many of the patchwork blocks featured here and in other books, magazines, and Internet reference.

Gather your supplies as listed on page 115 and decide whether to sew the blocks by hand or machine. Then work through the basic techniques with the easiest blocks—the Four-Patch and the Nine-Patch. As you build up your skills and confidence, make patchwork blocks with more complex designs, incorporating triangles and other shapes.

The most important thing to remember as you embark on this creative and dynamic hobby is that it's supposed to be fun! Be patient with yourself as you progress, and when you make mistakes, learn from them and move on. It's only fabric, and there's plenty more available. If it's easier for you to learn from watching someone, enlist another quilter to help you or look for quilt classes at local shops and adult schools.

Question 86:
I'm just starting. What should my first patchwork quilt be?

When you've got some basic blocks under your belt, think about creating one of the sampler quilts offered in this book. Sampler quilts provide an excellent way to learn the basics of patchwork and quilt design because you try many different blocks, each with its own construction characteristics. The diversity provides a continual challenge and you won't find yourself bored by repeating blocks.

Or you might just create several blocks and turn them each into mini-quilts or small quilted projects, like placemats, wall quilts and hot pads. I always encourage beginners to start with small projects that they can complete fairly quickly.

If you really want to make a large quilt, try working on a lap-sized quilt, around 50 inches by 70 inches. It will be easy to piece and quilt on your machine, and is perfect for draping over a couch, chair, or the end of your bed for a spot of color.

Another thought about working on your first or second project:

Use high-quality fabric that you're absolutely in love with. Do not expect to enjoy your project if you choose ugly fabric or if the fabric is poor in quality. If you're going to spend your time working on a quilt, you need to be proud of it when it's done, and you want to use it.

And finally, when you do make that first quilt or project, keep it for yourself. Save that friend's baby quilt or your parent's anniversary quilt for your second or third project. Years from now, when you're an accomplished quilter, you'll appreciate looking back with pride on your first quilt, no matter how it turns out.

Question 87:

What tools and materials will I need?

The simplest quilts are made from fabric, batting, and thread. Period. The basic tools used to work with these materials are scissors, cardboard for templates, hand needles, an iron, and an ironing surface. This is all you need to create a hand-stitched, hand-quilted patchwork quilt.

Other tools were designed to make patchwork faster, more accurate, easier to accomplish, and more

aesthetically pleasing. There are so many different tools in the quilt marketplace to experiment with and spend your money on. In fact, there seems to be an endless number of tools available to carry the job to completion.

A sewing machine is the primary time-saving tool for most quilters. A quilt can be made from start to finish using a sewing machine, or you can keep it just for certain tasks in the quilt's creation. Sewing machines range in price from $50 to the equivalent of a new car.

The rotary cutter is another tool to revolutionize quilting. It comes in all shapes and sizes, and some rotary cutters cut circles instead of straight lines. When used with cutting mats and rotary rulers, rotary cutters become the perfect quilting tool and enable quilters to cut fabric more precisely and quickly than scissors and cardboard templates.

ABOVE Rotary cutter, mat, and ruler.

Question 88:

Help! I'm trying to set up my work space...

When first starting out in quilting, many quilters settle for a dining room table with an ironing board set up nearby. This might carry you through a project or two, but you'll quickly find yourself dreaming of your perfect sewing space.

A well-designed sewing area will maximize your sewing time by allowing easy access to all of your tools and materials. It should have three main areas: a cutting area, a pressing/ironing area, and a sewing area.

If you're working by hand, your sewing area might be a comfortable chair or couch with very good lighting. If you're using a sewing machine, you'll need space for a table and chair, and an electrical outlet for your sewing machine.

Sewing machines serve quilters best when they are set flush into the work table or sewing cabinet. It allows your piecework to stay at the same level as the machine's needle, which helps prevent fabric distortion while you're sewing. It's also ergonomic — a fancy term meaning your body receives the least possible negative impact from your actions. Many sewing cabinets are made to allow your machine to sit flush with the table's top. But even if you don't have a sewing cabinet for your machine, you can still sew on your dining table or other surface. Make sure there's enough room to spread your work out, especially as the quilt grows.

Your cutting mat will partly dictate what your cutting area's size will be. Ideally, you'll be able to walk around the mat to cut at different angles. I love my kitchen island because for me, it's the perfect height for cutting. Dining tables also work well. Don't forget the need for good lighting.

Try to place your pressing/ironing station next to your cutting and/or sewing area. When quilting, you'll be pressing in between many sewing steps. You might want to place your ironing board at right angles to your sewing area. Lower your board to the same height as the sewing machine's surface. If you're blessed with a spinning work chair, you can swirl your chair to the ironing board to press the next piece.

Question 89:
Can you tell me what the parts of a patchwork quilt are?

- Blocks
- Borders
- Sashing
- Binding
- Back
- Top
- Batting
- Sleeve
- Label
- Cornerstone

- Cornersquare
- Inner Border
- Triangles
- Side Triangles
- Corner Triangles
- Alternate Blocks

Question 90:
What sewing machine should I buy?

Your choice of sewing machines is as personal as what toothpaste you prefer. Some features will definitely help your quilting along. If you have an unlimited budget for buying your sewing machine, the best quilting features include:

- Built-in walking foot;
- Large sewing machine bed for maneuvering large quilts;
- Fast straight-stitching speed for when your sewing ability allows for speedier stitching;
- Zigzag stitches for machine appliqué;
- Decorative stitches;
- Ability to lower the feed dog for machine quilting;
- An assortment of feet for specialized sewing tasks;
- An automatic needle threader;
- A built-in thread cutter;
- A built-in light;
- An extension table for when you sew-on-the-go with your machine

If you're on a tight budget, take a look at used machines. Look for used machines that have all of their attachments and an instruction book. Also, remember that a good repairman can fix almost anything.

If you're intending to buy a new machine, I strongly recommend you buy a sewing machine from a reputable local dealer.

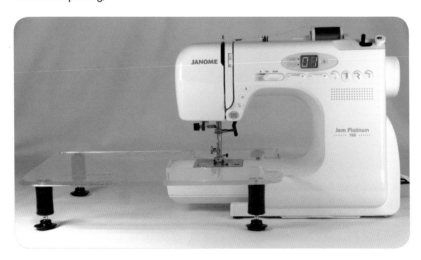

Question 91:
How do I take care of my sewing machine?

Sewing machines need regular oiling and cleaning, and for most machines you can do this yourself. Your machine's manual will probably have a section on how to clean and oil your machine, and your accessory kit might have screwdrivers and lint brushes to help get into those tight spots. Quilting generates a lot of lint, and you will need to regularly clear this from around the needle, the needle plate and the bobbin casing. If your manual doesn't give you the information you need to clean your machine at home, make a date with your dealer and ask for a quick tutorial on how to maintain your machine.

Even with consistent care on your part, your machine will need to have occasional tune-ups. If you're sewing frequently, plan on taking your machine in annually. With lots of use, your settings will loosen, and your dealer will need to make adjustments to the machine.

Question 92:
What accessories and attachments do I need to make patchwork quilts?

For quilt making, a ¼-inch foot should be your first purchase, if one was not supplied with your machine. Almost all quilts are made using ¼-inch seam allowances, and a ¼-inch foot provides an accurate seam guide for piecing the patches.

A built-in walking foot is great if your machine already has one. If not, consider buying a walking foot attachment that allows the top and the bottom fabrics to feed under the machine's foot at the same pace, helping to prevent puckers and tucks. It's especially handy when you're sewing on silky fabrics and

¼" foot

Darning foot

Single needle plate

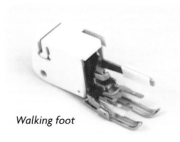
Walking foot

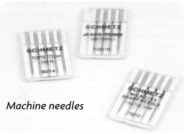
Machine needles

when you're machine quilting with a straight stitch.

A darning or free-motion foot is needed if you're going to try free-motion quilting at some point (and I encourage you to do so). This foot moves up and down with the needle's motion so that your quilt sandwich can move freely while you stitch.

A single needle foot, sometimes called a straight-stitch foot, accommodates the needle going straight up and straight down only, as opposed to side-to-side. It helps stabilize the fabric when you're straight-stitching. A single needle plate also helps to stabilize the fabric from beneath and is helpful for machine quilting.

You can never have too many machine needles. I buy them in bulk. Dull needles create all kinds of problems with your sewing, including skipped stitches, broken needles, and fabric snags.

If your sewing machine is very old or very basic, you may not be able to track down these accessories. Ask a dealer and check the Internet to see if there are alternatives from other companies that will work with your machine.

Question 93:
Is ironing a big deal in patchwork?

The difference between a great quilt and an "okay" quilt is often caused by the ironing and pressing performed during the quilt's construction. Your iron can smooth out troubled corners, make your quilt lie flat, ease in a patchwork piece that's just a shade too big, make crisper points and much more.

In quilt class, I see a lot of students who don't use enough pressure with their iron, as if they're afraid of it. Don't be. It's your friend, remember? You need to work that iron and work the fabric underneath.

Ironing and pressing are not the same actions. When ironing, the iron moves back and forth over the fabric. But in pressing, you use a simple up and down movement with the iron. Most quilters press their fabrics to avoid over-stretching the seams. That's fine, as long as you're using enough pressure to enable the heat to set the seams and smooth the fabric out.

Quilters debate the use of steam in quilt making. Because my sewing endeavors started with making clothes, not quilts, I learned early on that in most cases fabric responds better to moist heat. I am careful how I iron and press, making sure that I'm not stretching the fabric. I also prewash my fabrics before cutting, so shrinkage is not an issue. So the steam's always on in my iron, except when I'm working with paper patterns for paper/foundation piecing or working with delicate fabrics, such as silk and wool. Those are the only exceptions.

For cotton, your iron should be set at the hottest or near hottest setting. If you're working with silk, you'll need to lower the setting, and synthetics need the coolest settings to avoid melting. You don't have to spend a small fortune on an iron; inexpensive ones can work very well. But, again, it needs steam to get the best results.

94 What are the common quilt sizes?

95 How do I choose blocks for my quilt?

96 How can I effectively mix blocks?

97 Why do I need a sketchbook?

98 How much fabric do I need?

99 Can a computer help my designs?

100 Do I need a design wall?

101 Can you help with color choice?

102 What do I need to know about primary, secondary, and tertiary colors?

103 How do I use a color wheel?

104 What is the definition of hue?

105 What is the definition of shade?

106 What is the definition of tint?

107 What is the definition of tone?

108 What is the definition of value?

109 What is a monochromatic color scheme?

110 What is a complementary color scheme?

111 What is an analogous color scheme?

112 What is a split-complementary color scheme?

113 What is a triadic color scheme?

114 Where can I find examples of real-life color schemes?

DESIGNING PATCHWORK AND USING COLOR

Question 94:
What are the common quilt sizes?

There is no hard and fast rule about what size to make a quilt to fit a specific bed size or purpose. The following information gives you a starting point for minimum quilt sizes that work the best for a specific mattress or need.

Mattress sizes		Quilt sizes*	
Crib	28" x 52"	Baby	24" x 40" starting
Twin	39" x 75"	Lap	45" x 60" starting
Extra long twin	39" x 80"	Twin	50" x 85"
Full	54" x 75"	Full	65" x 85"
Queen	60" x 80"	Queen	70" x 90"
King	78" x 80"	King	90" x 92"
California King	72" x 84"		

*adjust according to preference for side drop and fold

Question 95:
How do I choose blocks for my quilt?

There's no set rule for selecting blocks for your quilt, but a fun way would be to select blocks based on common settings (Four-Patch, Nine-Patch, rectangles, etc.), themes (stars), or even the blocks' names. You can select one block, work with two repeating blocks that alternate in the design, or go for broke and use many different patchwork blocks in a sampler, or medallion quilt.

If you're concerned about how simple the patchwork blocks will be to construct, a good rule is that the more triangles your block has, the more difficult it will be.

When you alternate blocks in an arrangement, it can be useful to choose blocks with the same grid configuration. The blocks in this book are sorted by grid arrangement for this reason.

In a more traditional quilt design, the blocks are usually the same size and are arranged in an orderly fashion. A more contemporary approach is to use blocks of varying size arranged randomly, with filler blocks or patches in the spaces left by the irregular sizes.

Question 96:
How can I effectively mix blocks?

First, decide on the patchwork parts that will make up your quilt. What's bringing the blocks together for you; is it the grid arrangement? The theme? A color story? The color story means the main colors used in a quilt. The consistency of the colors helps to determine what patchwork blocks you choose.

When you've chosen your quilt's patchwork blocks, start considering the quilt's composition. Composition is the arrangement of the elements into a single design. When you look at any quilt, the deliberate choices made by the designer/quilter are the quilt's composition. Composition involves size, color, perspective, texture, balance, overall effect, and the weight of individual elements. A good composition employs balance to achieve harmony.

Balance is when the visual components (composition) of a quilt work together to create a harmonious arrangement.

Symmetry is the easiest way to achieve balance. A quilt that has the elements of shape, texture, and color arranged symmetrically will appear more balanced to the viewer.

For a quilt with asymmetrical patterns and images, balance is harder to achieve and can seem subjective. But when achieved, asymmetrical balance is much more.

Radial balance is when a central image is surrounded in a regular fashion by other elements. A square medallion quilt with repeating but differing borders provides an example of radial balance.

Balance can be achieved by using variety in the quilt's elements, by creating depth with visual perspective, and through repetition.

Question 97:
Why do I need a sketchbook?

Sometimes quilt designs are best conquered with pen and paper. Also, your best inspiration often hits you at the most inconvenient times. Having a sketchbook with you is the solution to noting those moments.

Sketching patchwork blocks is easy. The sketches don't need to be perfect, start with a rough pencil sketch. Cameras are a perfect tool for capturing real-life ideas and inspiration. Print out the photos that grab you the most and tape them into your sketchbook.

Use graph paper when fleshing out an idea. Even if you're working on asymmetrical designs, graph paper provides an excellent way to judge the scale and balance of your composition.

If you're working with blocks and traditional settings, you can draw your quilt to scale, and this will help you when it comes time to calculate yardage and cutting needs.

When you draw out your master plan, use a dark pencil and the graph paper. Later, when you need to try out color schemes, you can photocopy the master plan and color the copies with your crayons and markers. Keep your work together so that you can refer to these sketches as the quilt develops.

Question 98:
How much fabric do I need?

Remember that every piece cut needs to include a seam allowance.

You are creating a simple Nine-Patch quilt using a 15-block setting. Each Nine-Patch block will be 12 inches finished. We will need two fabrics. Each "patch" in the Nine-Patch will be a finished size of four inches square. You will need five patches of Fabric A and four patches of Fabric B in Block One. Block Two will use four patches of Fabric A and five patches of Fabric B.

Block One has (40) total 4 ½-inch patches from Fabric A. There are (36) total 4 ½-inch patches needed for Fabric B. In Block Two, there are (28)

4 ½-inch patches needed for Fabric A and (35) 4 ½-inch for Fabric B.

Fabric A will need to be big enough to cut (68) 4 ½-inch patches. Fabric B needs to allow for (71) patches at 4 ½-inches. If your fabric is 40-inches wide, you'll be able to cut (8) 4 ½-inch patches from each strip. You will need (9) strips at 4 ½-inches of Fabric A, totaling 40 ½-inches of the length of Fabric A. If we're working with a 36-inch yard, you will need a little less than 1 ¼ yards of Fabric A. Fabric B also need (9) strips at 4 ½-inches, totaling 40 ½-inches of the length. Again, you will need a little less than 1 ¼ yards of Fabric B.

Question 99:
Can a computer help my designs?

Good quilt design software enables you to create blocks and appliqué images either from your imagination or from a block library included with the program. You can map out your quilt designs, save them, print them, calculate the yardage needed, experiment with different color schemes, resize the blocks and/or the quilt, use different settings and borders to enhance your quilt, incorporate fabric scans, and pretty much take whatever is in your head and turn it into a quilt design.

EQ7 (www.electricquilt.com), updated in 2010, is probably the most popular PC-based program available. It has fabric images and tutorial books galore so you can create intricate and accurate quilt designs. As of this printing, the Electric Quilt Co. works only with Microsoft Windows systems, but Mac-based quilters can partition their hard drive to operate EQ7 on a Windows program. This sounds technical, but the Electric Quilt Company will guide you, and there are many online sources of help.

Quilt-Pro Systems (www.quiltpro. com) has several design programs for both PCs and Macs. Quilt-Pro's software can print paper foundation blocks and template papers to use in your quilts. QuiltSOFT (www. quiltsoft.com) also serves PCs and Macs, and offers additional block libraries.

New software applications are being developed all the time. Another tech innovation evolving in the last year or so is the advent of iPod, iPhone, and iPad apps (applications for Apple's popular portable devices). There are apps for block dictionaries and technique tutorials. Calculators specific to quilting needs and inspirational apps are readily available.

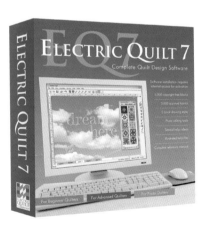

Question 100:
Do I need a design wall?

Design walls allow you to arrange your patches and blocks before you commit to sewing them together. Sometimes a boring quilt becomes exciting simply by using a different arrangement. Setting patchwork blocks on-point or using sashing to separate them can create a completely different quilt.

A classic design wall looks like a large flannel board mounted on a generous wall space. It can be as big as you wish, and should be as big as you can manage. The wall is covered with flannel or batting, which becomes a temporary sticking place for your fabric patches and blocks. If you're short on wall space, as many of us are, there are commercial and do-it-yourself options for design walls including roll-up flannel boards, paneled design walls that fold up in sections, and smaller design boards that can be tucked away when not in use. Even a large floor space that can be clearly viewed from above can become your design area.

Question 101:
Can you help with color choice?

Color theory, like most other design elements, can be studied and learned. Read through this chapter and commit to taking one or two color risks in your next project. Look through other books and magazines, and walk the aisles at quilt shows, noting the quilts you most admire for their color combinations. Start a sketchbook with pictures of these quilts and notes about your emotional impressions. When you identify your personal reaction, you can then manipulate your own designs to reflect what you wish them to express.

Another useful training tool comes from using crayons to sketch out block designs. Photocopy a line drawing of a block several times, and color it in different color schemes. There's no worry about mistakes here. It's all about how you see colors and how the colors interact.

Question 102:
What do I need to know about primary, secondary, and tertiary colors?

Primary colors are the foundation to all color families. Red and blue make purple, yellow and red become orange, and blue plus yellow equals green. Mix them all together, and earthy brown is your result.

Orange, purple, and green make the secondary colors. They are created from mixing equal amounts of their primary colors.

Tertiary colors are created when a primary color on the color wheel is blended with an adjacent secondary color. These colors include yellow-orange, magenta, and turquoise.

All of these are considered pure colors because they don't have any added black, white, or gray.

Question 103:
How do I use a color wheel?

One of the most useful tools for designing quilts is a color wheel, which allows you to see the interaction between colors, and help identify which color family a color belongs in: primary, secondary, or tertiary.

Color wheels are available from art supply stores and many quilt shops. Each color is a "spoke" on the wheel, and they are arranged in a rainbow pattern (red, orange, yellow, green, blue, and violet, with the tertiary blends in between). Each of these

colors is shown in its pure form, without the addition of black, white, or gray.

Question 104:
What is the definition of hue?

The term "hue" refers to the color itself, regardless of whether it's blended with black, white, or gray. A red hue can be dark, like maroon, or light, like pink. Greens can range from mint to forest, but their hue is always green.

Question 105:
What is the definition of shade?

When black is added to a pure color, it produces a shade. (Think "shadow" to remember shade.) Even tiny amounts of black will change a color's appearance, offering a change of mood.

Question 106:
What is the definition of tint?

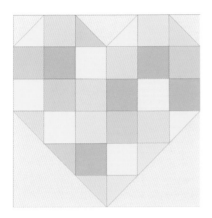

When white is added to a pure color, it produces a tint. Pastels are all tints, and we know them to be soft and gentle and to be soft and gentle to use.

Question 107:
What is the definition of tone?

When gray is added to a pure color it produces a tone. The word to remember here is "muted." The soft, suede-like effect of tones evokes a sense of quiet and peace, or the reflection of winter.

Question 108:
What is the definition of value?

Value refers to how light or dark a color is. Beginner quilters often find themselves drawn to medium-value colors because they feel safe and easier to work with. But it's important to incorporate a full complement of colors, if your quilt is not to be quiet and dull. Challenge yourself to pick a wide range of values in your fabrics and vary the amounts of each.

In the mid-1990s, "watercolor quilts" became a popular trend in quilting. These quilts started with different prints of all kinds cut into small pieces and identified by their value. Then the quilt was designed working with the pieces' values only. The resulting quilts looked like Impressionist paintings, or watercolors. Quilters used a special tool called a value lens to determine how light or dark the fabrics were in comparison with others. These lenses are readily found in quilt shops and come in red or green.

Question 109:

What is a monochromatic color scheme?

Color schemes are arrangements of colors. Monochromatic color schemes feature one hue, for instance blue, but use its many tints, shades, tones, and values to achieve contrast, texture, and mood.

Question 110:
What is a complementary color scheme?

Colors directly across from each other on the color wheel (blue-orange, red-green, purple-yellow) are complementary colors.

Using complementary colors in a quilt's design should be done with care, as the effect can be visually jarring. Pure green and pure red together in a quilt can overwhelm the design and give the appearance that the colors are competing with each other. However, consider how beautifully a soft pink and deep hunter green play together in a

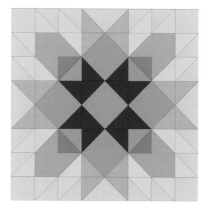

design, each color with its own role to play and neither overshadowing the other.

Question 111:
What is an analogous color scheme?

An analogous color scheme uses two or more colors placed next to each other on the color wheel. Picture a quilt made using only those colors starting at green and ending at violet. Using all of the shades, tints, tones, and values available to work with, this quilt could pack a dramatic punch, or stay subtle and soft.

Question 112:
What is a split-complementary color scheme?

A split-complementary color scheme uses an analogous color scheme of any size variation (three colors, five colors, or seven colors, for instance) plus the complementary color from the opposite side of the color wheel. Nature often plays with this scheme in the colors found in flowers—roses are a classic example with their beautiful range of reds, pinks, peaches, and yellows set off against the green of their leaves and stems.

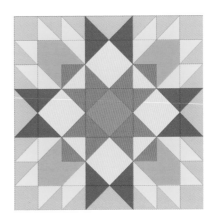

Question 113:
What is a triadic color scheme?

A triadic color scheme uses three colors equally spaced along the color wheel, such as red, yellow, and blue, or purple, orange, and green. Again, the key to working with these colors comes from the variety and proportions of tints, tones, shades, and values used in the design.

Question 114:
Where can I find examples of real-life color schemes?

The answer to this question starts right outside your front door. Everywhere you look in nature and the man-made world, you'll be struck with examples of color schemes that work (and some that don't). Flowers are an obvious source of inspiration, but architecture, landscapes, modern art, animals, the changing sky, food, people, and almost anything else can become inspiration for a color scheme.

When you're hunting for your color inspirations, it's prudent to be armed with a camera and sketchpad. When using your camera, remember that most of what you're shooting will be better served by getting in close to the subject. Also, pay attention to the time of day and how the natural light may alter the wall's coloring. Sunlight, shade, and moonlight can radically change a subject's color, and what repels you in full light might seduce you in shade.

It is important thing to train your eye to take in the colors surrounding you. Always look at both the big picture and the details. Compose your quilts the same way you would your photographs because the composition determines the balance of colors to be used. When you really like an image, note the colors of course, but also the textures and the amount of each color.

Finally, seek out sources on the Internet for learning about color. Pantone, one of the world's leading color forecasting companies, offers lots of color information on their Web site, www.pantone.com.

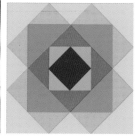

115 Can you tell me about fabric?

116 Is cotton the only fabric used in patchwork?

117 How do I prepare my fabric?

118 What are "grain" and "bias"?

119 What is the definition of selvage?

120 Do you have any tips for choosing fabrics for my patchwork?

121 How big is XX cut of fabric?

122 What is a fat quarter?

123 What is a fat eighth?

124 What are rotary cutters?

125 How do I safely change my blade?

126 Do they make left-handed rotary cutters?

127 What's the best way to hold a rotary cutter while cutting?

128 What are rotary mats and rulers?

129 Can't I just use cardboard templates?

9

CHOOSING AND CUTTING FABRIC

Question 115:
Can you tell me about fabric?

For quilters, fabric is our medium for creating our art, regardless of the style in which we work.

Most traditional quilts are made from high-quality woven cotton, but quilts can also be made from velvet, wool, silk, cotton flannel, and other textiles. Victorian Crazy quilts used pretty much any scraps of fancy fabrics the quiltmaker could get her hands on. Wool quilts are a wonderfully warm and cozy alternative to cotton for cold-weather areas. Silk is a standout choice for adding dash to a quilt and many art quilters use it in their creations.

Nevertheless, cotton remains a strong choice for patchwork, especially for beginners, partly because it's so plentiful and the variety of prints and styles available is so wide and partly because cotton is, in most instances, the easiest fabric to manipulate, sew, and press.

Question 116:
Is cotton the only fabric used in patchwork?

Patchwork quilts can be made from other kinds of fabrics (see above), but the most traditional look comes with using cotton.

Lightweight wool, silk, linen, and other natural fibers can be interesting substitutions for your quilt. Synthetics don't always wear well over time and can be difficult to handle. If you're using silk, be aware that many silks need to be

ABOVE Fancy fabrics.

stabilized before using or they will shred in your quilt. There are many fusible stabilizers and interfacings readily available for reinforcing your beautiful silks.

Question 117:
How do I prepare my fabric?

We're talking about cotton here; wool, silks and other fabrics follow different rules. Make you own decision about prewashing, but whenever possible, I prewash my fabrics. The reasons are:

- Some shrinkage will occur with most cottons, and I'd rather get it out of the way beforehand;
- Washing removes any chemicals and sizing on the fabrics, which gives me a better sense of how the fabric feels and handles;
- And lastly, washing will remove any latent dyes before they have the chance to run in the finished quilt.

To prewash fabrics, I run them through a washer and dryer just as I do my T-shirts. I try to iron them right away, but if not, I fold them carefully. I normally spray-starch my fabrics when ironing. Starch stabilizes the fabric's threads making cutting more accurate, discourages fabric from stretching out of shape, and stubborn creases are easily tamed. A light starch is fine. Or try soaking the fabrics in a homemade mix of starch in the tub, then hang them out to dry. The reason many quilters don't prewash their fabrics is that they don't mind the small amount of shrinkage after washing. Also, today's dyes are usually extremely stable, and they're willing to take a chance.

Question 118:
What are "grain" and "bias"?

"Grain" refers to the horizontal and vertical directions of the threads in the fabric's weave. When the fabric is folded or cut along the grain, the grain becomes the straight-line guide. When fabric is said to be "straight of grain," its grain line runs lengthwise; "cross grain" runs parallel to the fabric's width. Some quilt shops will tear fabric (instead of cutting) along the grain.

A fabric cut on the bias has been cut along the grain's diagonal at a 45-degree angle to the weave, which creates a cut edge that is unstable and stretchy. Bias cuts provide more flexibility when the fabric needs to be sewn or folded along a curve. Many quilters cut their binding strips along the bias to maneuver binding along a serpentine (curved/waved) border. Bias-cut strips work well in appliqué when you might need shapes that require more give.

When cutting pieces for most straight-edged patchwork, cut along the grain to prevent the pieces from fraying and to ensure accuracy.

Question 119:

What is the definition of selvage?

"Selvage" is the long, finished edge of the fabric. The width of the fabric is measured between the two selvages. Most fabric companies use the selvage to print the name of the fabric and its designer. You might also see a series of colored dots on the selvage. These are the colors found in the fabric's print, and can be very helpful when matching fabrics.

Keep some of the selvage until your project is complete. If you run out of fabric midway through a project, this information can help you track down a further supply.

Most cotton quilting fabrics are milled on looms that create fabric 44-inches wide. (The industry provides a safety margin by figuring fabric is 40-inches wide.)

ABOVE Selvage information.

Question 120:
Do you have any tips for choosing fabrics for my patchwork?

The three main things to consider when selecting fabric for your next quilt project are color, balance, and texture. You should work around a "focus fabric." A focus fabric is usually a print containing several or many colors. For the example pictured, a pretty ocean print with sea turtles serves as the focus print, because it has lots of colors and a good all over pattern. The background color will normally serve as your main color, but if there's a higher proportion of another color, you might choose that instead. The remaining colors offer you a palette from which to select your other fabrics. These don't have to match exactly the colors in the focus fabric so long as they blend well together.

To achieve balance with the colors, (which does not mean that every color is used in equal quantities,) look at the percentage of each color used in the focus fabric print. If green is only a small part of the overall color scheme, green fabric should not be given a prominent place in your quilt's design. Instead, use it as an accent color that

ABOVE The print's background color helps the selection of the other fabrics.

enhances the other colors. But if yellow amounts to about one-third of the focus fabric, then it can and should feature prominently in your fabric selection.

The last factor when selecting your fabrics has to do with texture. Each fabric's print has a "texture," and your quilt will be much more interesting when you use different print textures. A small, dotted print offers a texture that is generally easy on the eye, while a bold paisley can dominate a design.

You also need to consider the size of the print in relation to the patch it's used for. If you're unsure about the colors and textures for a quilt, use your sketchbook and crayons to try out colors, and make a sample block with the fabrics.

Question 121:
How big is XX cut of fabric?

⅛ yard: 4 ½" X 40"
¼ yard: 9" X 40"
⅓ yard: 12" X 40"
½ yard: 16" X 40"
⅔ yard: 24" X 40"
⅞ yard: 31.5" X 40"
1 yard: 36" X 40"

ABOVE Jelly rolls are pre-cut fabrics.

Question 122:
What is a fat quarter?

A fat quarter describes a very popular cut of fabric that runs approximately 18 inches by 20 inches. Fat quarters came about because a standard quarter yard of quilt fabric, which runs 9 inches by 40 inches, is an awkward size to use in quiltmaking. By instead taking a half yard of fabric (18 inches by 40 inches), folding it across its width (selvage to selvage), and cutting it in half again along the fold, you end up with the same area as the standard quarter yard in a more useable form. So a half yard of fabric yields two fat quarters. A good quilt shop will cut a fat quarter from a bolt when asked.

For these measurements, figure the fabric's width (from selvage to selvage) is 40 inches. As already said, there may be some variation of that width, as much as four inches.

Fat quarters are very popular with quilt designers because many stores and fabric companies package fat quarters in pre-coordinated bundles to make fabric selection easier. There are scores of book dedicated solely to using fat quarters in quilts. Fat quarters are also great to use in small craft projects and make a great gift.

Question 123:
What is a "fat eighth"?

Smaller than a fat quarter, a fat eighth is a cut 9 inches by 20 inches. Fat eighths are handy for novelty quilts and scrap quilts, though not as flexible as the fat quarter.

Question 124:
What are rotary cutters?

Rotary cutters have changed forever the way quilters cut their fabric. They enable patchwork pieces to be sliced and diced in no time at all. Please be aware that rotary cutters are very sharp and can be dangerous if not used with care.

Choose a rotary cutter with a safety mechanism. Olfa makes a widely available rotary cutter with a retractable blade. With the older kind of rotary cutters, you have to flip a latch to cover the blade. If you have to use this kind of rotary cutter, make it your habit right from the start to always flip the latch, even if you will soon be cutting again.

ABOVE Different rotary cutters.

Keep your rotary cutter away from children at all times, both while you're working and when you're done. Dull blades are a danger as well. They will make you push harder, which reduces your control over the blade. A nicked blade leaves gaps in your cutting.

Question 125:
How do I safely change my blade?

Most common rotary cutters hold the blade in place with a nut and washer. To remove the blade, the nut is unscrewed on the opposite side of the cutter from the blade.

To be safe, change your blades only when you won't be distracted. It's very easy to cut yourself with an exposed blade. Place the rotary cutter on a stable surface, blade side down. Unscrew the nut, remove the washer and place them next to you in the order you've removed them. Carefully turn the cutter over so

that the blade is uppermost and lay it on the surface for support. There is probably a cover on the blade that will lift off. Your blade is now loose. Very carefully, slide the blade off the handle, making sure that your hand doesn't inadvertently close over the exposed blade. Again, safety is the most important concern. The old blade needs to be disposed of safely by putting it into something solid.

Take the new blade from its case, place it on the cutter's handle and secure it with the blade cover.

1. Unscrew nut.

2. Place nut, washer and cover down in order removed. Dispose of used blade.

3. Replace blade with new one and reassemble cover, washer, and nut.

4. Carefully check to make sure all parts are tightly screwed and moving.

Choosing and Cutting Fabric

Again, carefully turn the cutter over (the blade can slip!) and replace the washer and then the nut, tightening the nut until it's secure. Your blade is now ready to use.

There are many different makes and models of rotary cutters on the market, but most will use a system similar to this to change a blade. If you're unsure, there should be instructions on the packaging of either the cutter or the extra blades.

I store my old machine needles and rotary blades in a small coffee tin with a plastic lid that has a hole in it. When it's full, it gets tossed safely into the trash. There are also some groups that use dull rotary blades for working with leather, which means you can recycle your blades.

Question 126:
Do they make left-handed rotary cutters?

Rotary blade left hand.

Rotary blade right hand.

Most standard rotary cutters have the blade on either side, so it can be changed to accommodate a left- or right-handed person. If you're right-handed, the blade should be fitted on the left side of the cutter, so that it butts up against the right edge of your rotary ruler.

If you're left-handed, fit the blade on the right side of the rotary cutter and butt the blade against the left edge of the rotary ruler. Simply switch the blade to the other side and make sure you maintain the order of the washer, blade, and nut.

Choosing and Cutting Fabric   143

Question 127:
What's the best way to hold a rotary cutter while cutting?

First, when you're holding the rotary cutter, wrap your entire hand around the cutter's handle. DO NOT place your finger along the handle toward the blade. It places your finger too close to the exposed blade and one slip can slice your finger. If you're applying steady pressure to the blade, you will be in control of the blade at all times.

Always use a self-healing rotary cutting mat, which has a grid to help you and a surface which grips the blade, offering additional safety.

Never drag the rotary cutter toward you as you cut the fabric. Cut away from your body at all times. Don't saw through the fabric — the cut should be one smooth, continuous motion.

Start with your fabric neatly pressed, and folded if necessary. Line up the straight, folded edge of your fabric along one of the cutting mat's bottom grid lines. With your ruler placed on top of the fabric, start from the fabric end closest to you and push the blade away from you in one continuous motion. If the piece of fabric is long, you might have to stop halfway through the cut, realign the ruler, and continue. Make sure the fabric is always on the mat. Apply a steady and firm pressure to the rotary cutter—you need to be in control of that cutter at all times.

BELOW Holding a rotary cutter.

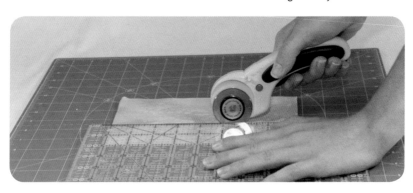

Question 128:
What are rotary mats and rulers?

Holding the ruler correctly is the key to successful cutting. When you're choosing your first rulers, go for a 6 X 24 inch ruler or an 8½ X 24 inch ruler. These sizes will cover most of your cutting needs. For your next rulers, look for a 12 X 15 inch square and possibly a 4 X 14 inch ruler. Make sure that you can read the numbers and see the lines clearly.

To help prevent slipping, sandpaper dots on the back of the ruler grip the fabric as you cut. Another tool to help control rulers is a handle with suction cups to grip the ruler. These are also found in quilt shops.

With practice you won't need extra tools. Starting with a long ruler, put your left hand to the left side of the ruler (if you're left-handed, switch sides through these instructions), and drop your pinkie over the ruler's edge. Make sure your fingers are nowhere near the ruler's right edge. Start cutting the fabric from the bottom to the top of the ruler. Make sure the side of your rotary cutter's blade is right up against the ruler's edge. You can angle the rotary blade just slightly away from the ruler's edge to get clean cut.

Question 129:
Can't I just use cardboard templates?

Quilters used to make templates from cardboard. Now, we usually use rotary cutters and measurements for cutting. But templates are still used in appliqué, although they tend to be made from template plastic and drawn with permanent markers. Cardboard is still an option, but if you're cutting lots of shapes with a cardboard template, it will wear down quickly. Template plastic is more durable. Simply trace the shape onto the template plastic with a permanent, extra-fine line marker. Carefully cut the shape from the plastic, making sure your lines are steady and nick-free. Then, using the kind of marking pen or pencil which can be removed later, trace the shape onto your fabric, and cut out with a rotary cutter and mat or with scissors.

130 What is the best thread to use?

131 What about sewing machine needles?

132 What about my bobbin?

133 What is thread tension?

134 Are pins really necessary?

135 How do I perfect my ¼ inch seam?

136 How do I piece a patchwork block?

137 How do I nestle my seams?

138 How do I press my seams?

139 What are dog ears?

140 Can I strip-piece my patchwork blocks?

141 How do I sew curved pieces?

142 Can I use paper piecing?

143 What are Half-Square and Quarter-Square triangles?

144 How do I calculate the size of triangles from squares?

10
MACHINE PIECING

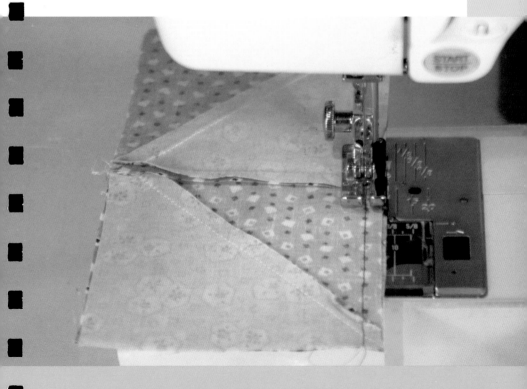

Question 130:
What is the best thread to use?

Most quilters prefer to machine-piece with a high-quality cotton thread. Aurifil, Gutterman, J.P. Coats, Mettler, Superior, and YLI all work well, and these are just some of the brands available. Many quilters prefer using all-cotton thread because most quilts are made solely from cotton.

Stock up on threads in a small selection of neutral colors, and you'll have most of your projects covered. As long as there isn't too much contrast between the colors, the thread will blend into the fabric.

If the thread is old, it can break as it moves through the machine. The same goes for thread that is not high quality. If your thread starts breaking, replace it.

For piecing, I use a fine to extra-fine thread, 40 to 60 weight (the larger the number, the finer the thread.) Long-staple Egyptian cotton is always nice. Longer staple will result in less fringing and lint.

Question 131:
What about sewing machine needles?

Most standard cotton thread is best served by a "sharps" needle (one with a sharp point) sized 70/10, 80/12, or 90/14. The first number is the European listing, and the second number is the American listing. All mainstream needles are marked with both numbers. The smaller the numbers, the smaller the needles. For thinner-weight threads (50 or 60 weight), use a 70/10 needle if you can. If not, the 80/12 will work.

Machine quilting and specialty threads (e.g. metallics, lightweight silks, denim, or rayon) require different needles, but for basic piecing, sharps will suit you fine.

You must change your needles frequently. The harder your needle has to work, the quicker it will dull.

Question 132:
What about my bobbin?

Sewing machines work by looping two threads together to create a chain stitch that links two or more pieces of fabric together. The thread on top is called the top thread. The bottom thread is called the bobbin thread. Bobbins are small spools of thread usually loaded in the machine's base or on the front side of the machine.

For basic machine-piecing, you're fine using the same thread for the top thread and in the bobbin, especially if you're using the finer, high-quality threads I recommend for piecing. Bobbins seem to prefer thinner threads. At the start of your project, wind at least two bobbins.

Bobbins, especially plastic ones, will wear out over time. Small nicks and scratches can catch the thread as it moves off of the bobbin and through the machine. If you find your thread is breaking or your machine is jamming, you might need to replace the bobbin. Fortunately, bobbins are easy to replace through the manufacturer or from a fabric store's notions racks. Wind your bobbin following the directions in your sewing machine's handbook. Keeping the proper tension during the winding is important. This is separate from the sewing tension, explained in Question 133. If there's any problem during the winding, such as the thread becoming loose or wound around the spindle that holds the bobbin, remove all of the thread from the bobbin and start over. Loose bobbin thread can jam the bobbin casing and create a tangled mess in your machine.

The bobbin casing also has a tension setting. In some machines the casing is removable; in others it rests permanently in the machine, and some types of specialty thread might require a tension adjustment to the bobbin casing. You'll need to refer to your sewing machine manual and be sure to make any adjustments to the casing slowly and in very small steps. It's easy to over-adjust tension on a sewing machine.

BELOW Bobbins and casing.

Question 133:
What is thread tension?

The pull on both the top thread and the bobbin thread as it passes through the sewing machine is called the tension. Most sewing machines have a tension dial on the front of the machine with numbers ranging from zero to nine. Standard sewing on a machine in good working order will generally use a tension of between 3.5 and 6.

You'll know when your tension is off because the threads will either look like they're lying above the fabric or they will pull so tightly that the fabric puckers. Adjust the tension dial in very small steps. It shouldn't take much to see an improvement in the stitching.

If the stitching doesn't improve, take the machine to the dealer or a reputable repairman. Sewing machines, like most complex machinery, need to be tuned regularly, and if your machine has not been serviced for a year, that could be the problem.

If you are machine-quilting, sewing very thick or very thin projects, or are using specialty threads in your machine, you will probably need to adjust the tension for these weights and fibers. Again, make slight adjustments each time, and when you find the perfect tension for your combination of project and material, write it down where you'll be able to locate the information easily.

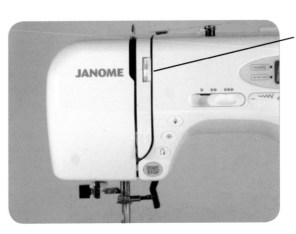

LEFT Tension dial on sewing machine.

Question 134:
Are pins really necessary?

There are different pins for different tasks—use the pins that are appropriate for the job they need to do. I prefer working with glass-head pins about 1 ½ inches long. I also have silk pins, which are short and very fine, and appliqué pins, which are even shorter. Large safety pins for basting and grouping pieces should also be in your sewing kit, and a pin cushion is helpful.

To pin fabric patches before sewing them together, line up the edges exactly, and insert your pin perpendicular to the edge. In other words, create a right angle between your pin and sewing line. If you're pinning large pieces of fabric together, such as a border to a quilt top place your pins no further than 3 inches apart.

As you're sewing the fabric together, do not sew over the pins! Sew along the seam, stop just before the pin starts traveling under the foot, and remove the pin to place it in a pin cushion.

Question 135:
How do I perfect my ¼-inch seam?

Almost nothing in patchwork is more important than an accurate ¼-inch seam. When you piece a traditional patchwork block, the ¼-inch seam must be accurate if the block is to finish the correct size.

If your seams are off by even ¹⁄₁₆ inch, you can find yourself inches short by the time you sew your blocks together into rows. If your seams are randomly inaccurate, your patchwork blocks might not even come together.

There are several different ways to make sure that your ¼ inch is a true ¼ inch. Start by buying a ¼-inch foot for your sewing machine; there are generic ¼-inch feet available through large notions retailers. You'll need to know which will fit your machine, and this is usually determined by whether the shank (the arm holding the machine's feet) is long or short. Bernina machines have a completely different shank style, and you may need an adapter.

Some ¼-inch feet have a lip on the right edge of the foot that follows the fabric's edge. These are helpful and worth the purchase if your machine can use one.

Another way to work this, is to take a piece of paper with a straight edge and draw a line from top to bottom along the right-hand edge at exactly a ¼ inch. (A rotary ruler is the easiest way to measure.) Place the paper under your sewing machine needle, lowering the needle on the right edge of the drawn line. Then, without any thread in the machine, sew along the line until you're halfway down the paper. Stop sewing and make sure your needle is down in the paper. Carefully stick a strip of masking tape on the

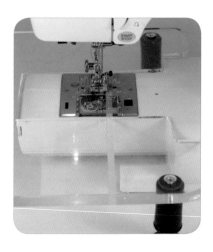

machine's bed, along the right edge of the paper. Make sure the tape sits from the front of the machine's bed to the back. When you remove the paper, the tape is now placed a ¼ inch.

Question 136:

How do I piece a patchwork block?

Most quilt patterns and books provide instructions on how to piece a patchwork block. For simple patchwork involving squares, triangles, and rectangles, you'll put two patches of fabric right sides together, lined up along their straight edges. Place this unit under your sewing machine foot and, following your ¼-inch guide or foot, stitch from the unit's top to the bottom. If you use a small stitch

length, around 1.8 or 2 on most machines, you'll probably not need to backstitch your first couple of stitches. A backstitch provides extra security against a seam splitting during pressing and handling. To backstitch start stitching about a ½-inch below the unit's top with a reverse stitch, get to the top edge of the unit, and then start stitching the unit in the forward stitch.

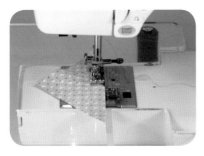

1. Place two patches of fabric, right sides together and lined up along right edge, under foot and align to ¼ inch mark or foot.

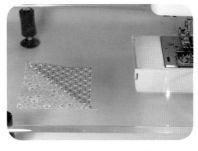

2. Sew patches from top to bottom. Press seam to darker patch unless told otherwise.

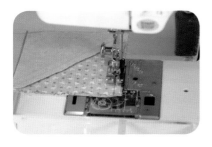

3. Sew two patches, right sides together and lined up along right edge. Repeat on second set of patches.

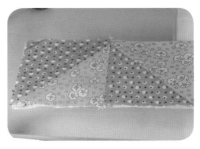

4. Press the seams for the two sets in opposite directions. If the top set has its seams pressed to the left, then the bottom set should have its seams pressed to the right.

5. Pin the two set together and nestle the seams at the middle so they feel completely settled into each other. Sew. Press seam in either direction.

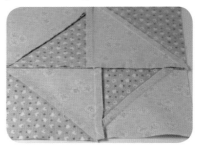

6. From the back side, a perfect Pin-wheel block.

Question 137:
How do I nestle my seams?

When two seams pressed in opposite directions are sewn together accurately, one seam will sit to the right of the seamline and one to the left of the seamline, creating a perfect cross where the four pieces of fabric come together. This cross, called nestling, allows the flattest possible joining of the seams. Aim for perfect nestling in all of your seams, and you'll have perfect intersections on the quilt's front. Pinning carefully will help achieve this.

ABOVE Learn how to perfect your nestled seams.

Question 138:
How do I press my seams?

Seam pressing is another important technique for creating accurate quilts, and, while it is not difficult, these are some tips for doing it well. Unlike clothing construction where seams are usually pressed open, in quilting you'll press most seam allowances to one side of the seam. Whenever possible press the seam allowance toward the darker fabric so that it doesn't show through a light-colored fabric. If you're using

a quilt pattern, follow the pattern's pressing instructions, if there are any. Sometimes more accurate piecing of the block is accomplished by using specific pressing directions (it's that nestling thing again).

To press your seams, gently open the fabric piece and place it right-side down on the ironing surface. With the long side of the iron, smooth the seam in your chosen direction. Start moving the iron not on the seam but on the fabric next to it. Check that there are no creases on the right side of the fabric. If there is a crease, re-press from the wrong side again, not the right side as this could put seam-line impressions on the front of the quilt.

When pressing edges that are cut on the bias, take great care not to stretch the edges with the weight and heat of the iron. Bias edges are unstable because they are cut through the threads instead of with the direction of the threads.

Starch is the secret weapon of many a quilter, and it always amazes me how many seasoned quilters don't take advantage of this wonderful aid. Whether you mix your own or buy it in a spray can, starch adds body to cotton fabrics and gives the iron that extra push of power. It sets the seams firmly and helps stabilize the threads, especially if you're working on bias edges which are "looser" by nature.

Because I prewash all of my fabrics before cutting and piecing, I liberally use steam in my iron, which also gives the iron more power. Steam can be used with or without starch.

Question 139:
What are dog ears?

Sometimes, after you've pieced a unit and pressed its seam open, you see a small piece of the seam sticking out from the unit's edge. This is called a dog ear and happens mostly with triangles and other unusual shapes. Just trim the seam to the edge of the unit's intended shape and move on to the next step.

Question 140:
Can I strip-piece my patchwork blocks?

Strip-piecing is the first step in assembly-line quilting, which is a great way to save time when making a quilt. And because patchwork quilt designs often use repeating blocks, you can rip through the blocks' construction by strip-piecing.

When strip-piecing, line up your fabric sets and run them through your machine one after another. Do not raise or lower the presser foot; just feed the next set under the needle. When you're done with the line-up, snip the threads between each set to separate them, and press.

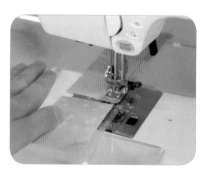

ABOVE To strip piece, line up your pairs of patches and feed each pair, one at a time, under the machine's foot and needle. Don't cut the pairs apart until all have been sewn.

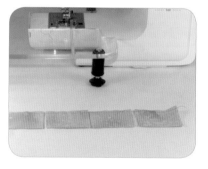

ABOVE The final chain or strip of patches can now be cut apart and pressed open. Strip piecing saves time!

Question 141:
How do I sew curved pieces?

For curved piecing, as in Drunkard's Path, or New York Beauty, pins will become your lifesaver. Use as many pins as you need to hold the pieces in place. In most traditional curved piecing, one piece of fabric will remain flat and the other may need to be clipped for successful piecing. The concave piece, which has an outside curve, will usually need a few clips to make it spread open. The clips are tiny snips from the fabric's outside edge to just before the marked stitching line. Don't clip past the line as this would create a hole in the piece! The number of clips depends on the size of the piece and whether the curve is slight or extreme. Start with a couple and see if you can pin the curve well to the flat piece. If not, add a few more clips. Then start sewing along your seam, removing pins as you work. When done, press the seam and make sure there are no small puckers hiding in it.

LEFT Using a stiletto, skewer or some other long, pointed tool will help you with your curved piecing. With practice you won't even need to pin.

RIGHT The finished block should have a smooth curve. Clipping the seam allowance at regular intervals before pressing will enable the block to lie flat.

Question 142:
Can I use paper piecing?

With paper piecing (sometimes called foundation piecing), a paper pattern becomes a sewing guide for your patchwork block or unit. You sew the fabric to the paper pattern, which is later removed.

Paper piecing is best used for blocks requiring very sharp points, straight lines, and/or intricate piecing. Accomplished paper piecers can break down any image into tiny, straight-edged components to create complex motifs for their quilts. Paper piecing can save time as fabric does not need to be measured and cut accurately because the pattern is drawn on the paper.

The blocks offered here are constructed using traditional piecing techniques, but if you find yourself challenged by a block's construction, consider creating a paper-piecing pattern for the block.

Question 143:
What are Half-Square and Quarter-Square triangles?

A finished Half-Square triangle is a square bisected along one diagonal, with a different fabric on each side.

A finished Quarter-Square triangle is a square bisected along both diagonals. Traditionally, two fabrics are then arranged in pairs, opposite one another.

Half-Square and Quarter-Square triangles can be the bane of a quilter's life because it's very easy for the fabric patches to shift while cutting and piecing them together, especially if the triangles are small.

There are many tools on the market, from rulers to papers, designed to take the pain out of Half- and Quarter-Square triangles, because these simple arrangements are the base for many quilt blocks.

Quarter-square triangle.

Half-square triangle.

Question 144:
How do I calculate the size of triangles from squares?

To calculate the size of the square needed to produce two triangles that, when sewn together with a ¼-inch seam allowance, make a half-square triangle, add ⅞-inch to the measurement of the finished square. So, if you want a 1-inch finished square made up of two half-square triangles, you'll cut the triangles from a 1⅞-inch square.

To calculate the size of the square needed to produce four triangles that, when sewn together with a ¼-inch seam allowance, make a quarter-square triangle, add 1¼-inches to the finished measurement. So, if you want a 1-inch finished square made up of four quarter-square triangles, you'll cut four triangles from a 2¼-inch square.

When you cut the triangles from the squares, make sure the straight edges of the precut squares are aligned with the fabric grain.

145 How do I piece a Four-Patch block?

146 How do I piece a Flying Geese block?

147 How do I make Half-Square triangles?

148 How do I make Corner-Square triangles?

149 How do I make Quarter-Square triangles?

150 How do I sew Y-seams?

151 How do I piece long triangles?

152 How do I piece a Square in a Square?

153 How do I assemble a Pine Burr block?

154 How do I piece a Fan block?

11

BASIC BLOCK
CONSTRUCTION

Question 145:
How do I piece a Four-Patch block?

Patchwork blocks are made by sewing together cut pieces of fabric into sections and then sewing the sections into rows or groups. Many of the sections share common components. You could consider these the building blocks of patchwork. The following instructions represent the core sections of the majority of patchwork blocks. The techniques offered for these sections are the simplest we can offer, but like everything else in quilting, there are other techniques available for you to try if you're not happy with these results. Always make sure that you check your measurements for the sections where possible before sewing the sections into blocks. For instance, if a block is partly made from four Four-Patch blocks that need to be 3 ½ inches unfinished, you'll need to measure each Four-Patch block you make to be sure it's accurate.

1. For top row, sew B to A. For the bottom row, sew A to B. Press seams to darker fabrics.

2. Sew top row to bottom row.

3. Press the block with the seam going to either side.

Question 146:
How do I piece a Flying Geese block?

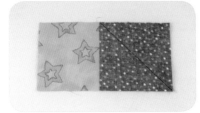

1. Place square on corner of rectangle, matching outer two edges of the square and rectangle, and draw diagonal line from outer corner to outer corner of square.

2. Sew along line, creating a Half-Square triangle. Check for accuracy, then trim triangle seam to ¼ inch. Open triangle and press seam to outer corner.

3. Repeat steps 1 to 2 on opposite rectangle corner.

4. Repeat to create one more Flying Geese unit.

5. Flying Geese block (made up from two units).

Question 147:
How do I make Half-Square triangles?

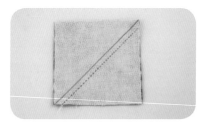

1. Layer square A with square B, right sides together with the lighter square on top. Draw a diagonal line on top square from corner to corner. Sew a ¼ inch seam along one side of drawn line.

2. Repeat sewing seam along other side of drawn line.

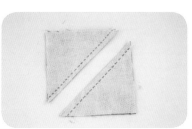

3. Cut along drawn line (makes two Half Square triangle units) and press each unit's seam to darker patch.

4. Check measurements of finished units to be sure they match the needed measurements of the square unit with seam allowances. For instance, a 3-inch finished square should measure 3 ½ inches.

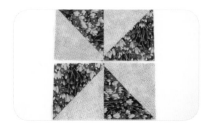

5. Half-Square triangles in a Pinwheel block.

Question 148:
How do I make Corner-Square triangles?

1. Place small square in corner of large square, right sides together, lining up two shared edges.

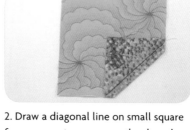

2. Draw a diagonal line on small square from corner to corner on the shared edges. Sew along line. Check the seam for accuracy, then trim triangle seam to ¼ inch.

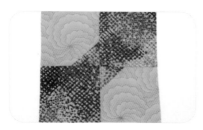

3. Fold triangle back to outside corner and press.

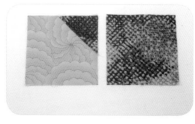

4. To make a bowtie block, add corner square unit to patterned unit.

5. Bowtie block.

Question 149:
How do I make Quarter-Square triangles?

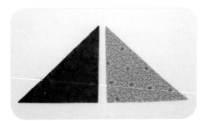

1. Cut squares for A and B. Then, cut A and B diagonally from corner to corner twice, as in an X pattern. You will now have 4 triangles from A and 4 triangles from B.

3. Sew one B triangle to one A triangle, following the illustration and press seam to darker triangle.

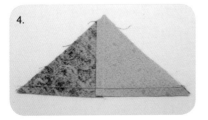

4.

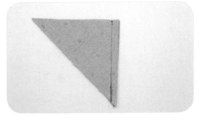

2. Cut squares for C. Then, cut each C diagonally from corner to corner once, creating 2 triangles from each patch, 4 altogether.

4. Sew 1 AB unit to long side of 1 C triangle. Press seam to C triangle. (Note: These instructions are specific to the Windmill block in Fig. 5 with four repeating quarter-square units. Adapt these instructions to the needs of the other blocks.)

5.

Question 150:
How do I sew Y-seams?

Y-seams don't have to be intimidating. The trick is to stop stitching exactly where needed, usually a ¼ inch from the fabric's edge. In this Attic Windows block, the two outer strips will create the illusion of a window pane. Use the pictures as guidance.

1. Line up the short edge of the trapezoid to one edge of the square, right sides together. Match the two right angles exactly and then use a pin to mark ¼ inch in from the other end of the strip, where your stitching will stop. With the square side facing up in the machine, stitch along the pinned edge just until where the pin is. Backstitch a couple of stitches, trim the threads, and press the seam to the trapezoid.

2. Line up the short edge of the other trapezoid to the unit, right sides together, and again use a pin to mark ¼ inch from the end of the stitching line. With the wrong side of the second trapezoid facing up in the machine, begin stitching along the edge, stopping just until where the pin is. Backstitch a couple of stitches, trim the threads and press the seam to the trapezoid.

3. Now sew the 90-degree angle that meets at the intersection of all three pieces. From the wrong side of the block, pin the two 90-degree angles together and carefully stitch to the where they meet. Press the seam to one side. Your Y-seam is now done.

Question 151:
How do I piece long triangles?

1. Cut triangles from templates.

2. Sew long edge of left triangle to left side of center triangle. Press seams to left triangle.

3. Sew long edge of right triangle to left side of center triangle.

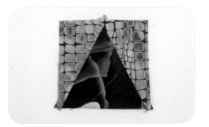

4. Press seams to right triangle. The finished long triangle.

Question 152:
How do I piece a Square in a Square?

1. Take square meant for the corner triangles and cut it in half on the diagonal twice, creating four Quarter Square triangles. Sew triangle to edge of square.

2. Press seam to triangle.
3. Repeat on other 3 sides.
4. Square in a square block.

1.

2.

3.

4.

Question 153:
How do I assemble a Pine Burr block?

1. A Pine Burr block (and its cousin, the Harlequin block) are pieced row by row from the bottom or largest end to the pointed top. Following the directions for piecing long triangles in Question 151, sew the bottom row of 5 triangles, followed by a row of 3 triangles (Pictures 1-5). See next page for Pictures.

2. Sew the row of 3 to the row of 5, then add a single triangle to the row of 3 following the orientation in the pictures. Repeat this three more times (Pictures 6 and 7).

3. Pin the long edge the pieced triangle to one edge of the center square. Sew and press seam to the square. Repeat on the other three sides (Picture 8).

4. Pin one long edge of the inset triangle along one long edge of the pieced triangle. Stitch from the outside to the inside, stopped ¼ inch from the end, similar to the Y-seam construction in Question 150. Press seam to pieced triangle. Repeat along other edge from the outside point to the inside point. Repeat on other three inset triangles (Picture 9).

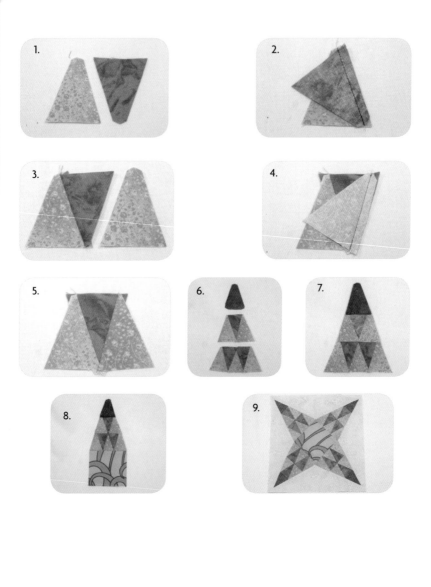

Basic Block Construction

Question 154:
How do I piece a Fan block?

1. Fold corners of blade to the wrong side of the blade's wide end to form a symmetrical point. Tack the ends down. Repeat for remaining blades.

2. Sew blades together in pairs, then sew pairs together until all 4 blades form fan shape. Press all blade seam allowances to one side.

3. Piece the groups together to form the fan. Appliqué the blades to background square A, by machine. Using thread matching the background square set the sewing machine's stitch to a narrow zigzag. Pin fan to background and stitch along edge of fan to background.

4. On circle, baste stitch about ⅛ inch along the outside edge of the circle leaving a long thread tail. Turn circle's edge under ¼ inch to the wrong side of the circle. Gently draw one thread in to slightly gather the edge and press in place. Then machine appliqué the circle to the center of the piece fan blades.

5. The finished Fan block.

155 How do I mark my rows?

156 How do I sew my rows together?

157 What is sashing for?

158 What is on point?

159 What is a border?

160 How much border fabric is needed?

161 How do I sew a straight-cut border?

162 How do I sew a mitered border?

163 What about pieced borders?

12

ROWS AND BORDERS

Question 155:
How do I mark my rows?

It's important to be able to spread your entire quilt out, either on a design wall or the floor, so that you can arrange your blocks into rows as they will be in the finished quilt top. If using a pattern, you probably already know the final arrangement. If you're using your own design or are adapting a pattern, expect to arrange and rearrange the parts until you're happy. If you're frustrated with the result, leave it overnight and look again in the morning. Quilt design benefits from a well-rested brain.

When you've finished spreading out your blocks, borders, sashing, and any other pieces, you'll need to label your rows or sections so that you sew the parts together in the correct order. Working from the top left corner of the quilt, use small sticky notes and pins to label the rows. Pin the sticky marked "1" to the first block of the top row and then pick up the rest of the blocks in the row in order and place them under this block. Make sure you don't turn or twist the blocks. This stack becomes Row 1.

Label the next row "2" and continue this process to the bottom of the quilt, making sure the stacking is consistent. If individual blocks have a specific orientation, add a north/up-pointing arrow to the sticky note to show in which direction the block is to be held and sewn. Leave the sticky notes in place until the entire top is sewn together, just in case you need it for reference.

Question 156:
How do I sew my rows together?

When sewing rows together, make friends with your pins. Most traditional patchwork quilts have regular seam intersections, and pins will help to control the length of pieced fabric and accurately mark where your intersections need to be. As each row is sewn, lay it on the floor or design wall right-side up, in order, from quilt top to bottom. For traditional patchwork quilts made from rows of pieced blocks, press all the seams for Row 1 in the same direction. Then, press the seams for Row 2 in the opposite direction. Continue alternating the seam directions to the last row.

With the rows pressed and face up in the correct order, take Row 2 and flip it over, wrong-side up, onto Row 1. You won't have to move Row 1 at all. Both rows are now right sides together, and it's time to start pinning. If you've pressed the seams correctly, Row 1's seams should be nicely nestled with Row 2's seams. Pin at each intersection of the nestled seams, as well as at the start and end of the rows. Most blocks will be big enough to need another pin or two between the seams' intersections. You'll be pinning so that Row 2 is on top.

After you've pinned your rows, bring them to your machine and with Row 2 on top, backstitch the end for about an inch and then stitch forward being careful not to stitch over the pins but removing them as you sew. If you're sewing with the seam allowance to the right of the needle, you'll sew the row from the top's right side to the left. Go slowly and make sure you're following your ¼-inch seam allowance guides. When you reach the end of the row, backstitch again and remove the joined rows from the machine.

Bring the joined rows to your ironing board and press the seam you've just sewn in one direction. It won't matter which direction, but use the same direction for each row.

Question 157:
What is sashing for?

Sashing is a strip of fabric, sometimes pieced, that separates and/or frames the blocks. Not all quilts have sashing, but sashing is a useful design element for spacing out the blocks or adding more length or width to a quilt.

If sashing is pieced, it can create a secondary design in the quilt's top.

There is no set size for sashing, but it should enhance the overall effect of the quilt's design, and if sashing is too wide, it can detract from the impact of the blocks.

Question 158:
What is on point?

Setting your square blocks "on-point" means turning the blocks to the diagonal, or at a 45-degree angle, with the square's corners facing north, south, east, and west. For many blocks, this quarter turn changes the design completely.

You'll have to fill in the sides with triangles in order to turn your on-point blocks into a straight-edged quilt. You'll have two kinds of triangles to deal with: the corner triangles and the side triangles.

There are fancy formulas for calculating the size of the triangles, and the fractions frankly become tiresome; a chart is simpler. Cut the squares and then make one or two cuts diagonally to create two or four triangles respectively. These square sizes are rounded to the nearest ½

inch, and you will therefore need to trim the side triangles to meet the edges of the on-point blocks. Do this after you've pieced all of the blocks with the side triangles. Line your rotary ruler up to the block's points and trim the triangles' excess to the points. For the corner triangles, use a corner rotary ruler to square up the corners to the on-point blocks and trim. Then add borders as desired.

Question 159:
What is a border?

Borders are fabric strips that frame the assembled quilt top. They can be simple or decorative. Most are straight, but some are curved or scalloped. Many quilts have a series of different sized borders. A border can also be pieced. Borders can be symmetrical, asymmetrical, or combined with other elements. Some quilts are "made" by their phenomenal border designs. Don't discount the quilt's border when you're working on your design; it's an important part of the quilt.

Question 160:
How much border fabric is needed?

Beginning quilters often cut lengths of border fabric at the width they want, sew them to the quilt top so that they extend beyond the corners of the top and then hem back. But this can sometimes result in a wavy border if your quilt's measurements are even slightly off.

Instead, measure your quilt across the middle—length and width—and use these measurements as your guide for cutting the border lengths. Cut the border strips from the fabric's length, parallel to the selvage in order to avoid piecing border strips. If you need to cut from the fabric's width and piece the border strips, make sure your pieces are cut very straight and use a ¼-inch seam.

Question 161:
How do I sew a straight-cut border?

Starting with the border strips for the quilt's top and bottom, measure the width of the quilt top through the middle and cut your strips to this size. (If you're piecing the border, add seam allowances as needed.) Pin the border strips to the quilt. You might need to "ease" either the quilt top or the borders to make the edges meet. "Easing" is a dressmaker's technique where a shorter fabric is very gently stretched to fit a slightly longer piece of fabric. Sew the borders to the quilt's top and bottom edges. Press the seams in the direction of the border.

Now measure the quilt's length through the middle, including the top and bottom borders. Cut the border strips, pin the borders in place, and sew, easing where needed. Press the seams in the direction of the border, and your top is ready for quilting. You can add as many borders as you like using this method. Many quilts feature double borders of differing sizes.

Question 162:
How do I sew a mitered border?

Master a mitered border, and you'll look like a seasoned quilt pro in no time! These borders look especially great with directional or large-print fabrics. They take a little practice to get right, but they're worth the time.

Decide on your border's width. Calculate the length of your border strips by measuring through the middle of the quilt, top to bottom and side to side. To these measurements add the border's width times two. Then, add 4 inches to that number and cut/piece your border strips.If you want a 6-inch wide border, and your lengthwise measurement is 50 inches, calculate 50 plus 12 (6 inch width times two) plus 4 equals 66. So you'll cut/piece your border strip at 66 inches by 6 ½ inches. (The ½ inch is for the piecing seam allowance.) Find the center of your borders and the center of each side of your quilt top. Pin the top and bottom borders to the quilt top, matching the centers, right sides together. Sew from end to end, stopping a ¼-inch short of each end. Press the seams in the direction of the borders. Sew the side borders in the same way.

Bring your quilt to the ironing board. At one corner, extend the border out and press. For the overlapping border, fold the end under at a 45-degree angle on top of the extended border and pin in place. (Use a square ruler to make sure the corner is accurate.) Use a blind stitch to tack the angled border down to the extended border. Then trim the seam allowance and press the seam open.

Question 163:

What about pieced borders?

Pieced borders can vary widely according to your quilt's design, and it is therefore not possible to give precise instructions. But here are some suggestions.

1. Try using one of the patchwork blocks from your quilt's design in a smaller version and spacing them around the borders.
2. Use a patchwork block as a "cornerstone" for your quilt, placing it in one or more corners of the quilt with the border strips in between.
3. If your quilt's design includes blocks with repeating elements such as Half-Square triangles, consider making a border from those elements.
4. Symmetry is restful to the eye, but asymmetry is often more interesting. If you're used to working with a symmetrical border, play with asymmetrical alternatives.
5. Checkerboard patterns can make dramatic quilt borders.
6. You can also add other elements to your borders, such as piping, rickrack, or Prairie Points.

164 How much fabric do I need for my quilt backing?

165 Is there a special way to piece my backing?

166 Should I only use cotton for my backing?

167 What is batting, and what kind should I use?

168 What is a quilt sandwich, and how do I make one?

169 How do I baste a quilt?

170 What is spray basting and is it better?

171 What's the best way to make sure my finished quilt hangs flat?

172 What's the point of machine quilting my quilt?

173 What is longarm quilting?

174 How do I prepare to machine-quilt my quilt?

175 Are there special materials needed for machine-quilting?

176 What kind of thread do I use for the top stitching?

177 Should I use the same thread in the bobbin as on top?

178 What needles should I use?

179 Can I use invisible thread?

180 What is stippling?

181 What about feathers, ropes, and medallion patterns?

182 What about stencils and other set quilt patterns?

183 How do I mark my quilting patterns on my quilt top?

184 So how do I free-motion quilt?

185 How do I perfect my machine quilting?

186 How do I pull my threads out of sight on the back of the quilt?

13

PUTTING IT ALL TOGETHER

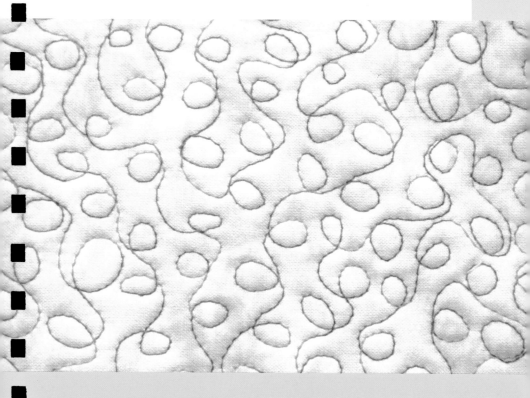

Question 164:
How much fabric do I need for my quilt backing?

Backing is the third layer of your quilt sandwich.

It can be as simple as a toning piece of fabric sewn, whole, to the quilt's back, or can be a pieced creation that could almost stand as a quilt top. Many fabric companies manufacture extra-wide backing fabric so that no piecing need be involved. Leftover scraps or unused blocks from the quilt itself can also be used in a backing.

To calculate how much backing fabric you will need, assuming that you're working with lengths of quilter's cottons at 40 inches wide, consider the following points:

- Make sure you include an extra 2 inches on each side of the quilt top to allow for any take-up in the quilting.
- If your quilt is 40 inches or less along two sides, you'll only need one length of backing fabric to cover the other measurement.
- If your quilt is larger, measure the entire quilt. Regardless of your quilt's orientation, take the smaller measurement and work from that. If the measurement is between 41 inches and 80 inches, you'll need two lengths of fabric to cover the back. If your measurement of the narrower side is between 80 inches and 120 inches, you'll need three lengths. Almost all quilts will fall into these ranges.
- To calculate the yardage needed, take the longer side and divide by 36. Round this up to the nearest half yard. Multiply that number by how many lengths you need to find your yardage.

Here's the math for a quilt that is 72 inches wide by 96 inches long:
1. 72 inches wide needs two lengths of fabric.
2. 96 divided by 36 is 2.66.
3. Rounded to the nearest half-yard, totals three yards.
4. Double that for the length needed.
5. It will take six yards to cover the quilt's back.

Question 165:
Is there a special way to piece my backing?

There is no set method to piece your backing, but you want to maximize the fabric you have. Assuming you have all the fabric needed, the easiest way until you're comfortable with the math involved is to sketch out a piecing plan for the back.

Draw the outline of the quilt's dimensions on paper and label the measurement in inches of each side. Figuring your backing fabric to be 40 inches wide, take the measurement of the narrowest side and divide that by 40. This is how many lengths of fabric you'll need for the backing. If your back is 70 inches wide, you'll need two lengths of the backing fabric. You'll sew one seam down the middle of two pieces of the backing fabric and trim the sides down later.

Alternatively you can work from the long side. If your quilt is 100 inches wide along that side, you'll need three lengths of fabric to cover the back. It doesn't matter which way you work as long as there is enough fabric to do the job.

Some quilters piece large leftover scraps of fabric together. Again, this is a numbers game, and you'll need to calculate what to sew and what

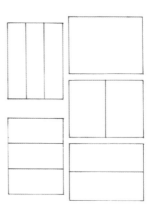

ABOVE Piecing backs.

you need. Sketch out the plan using the measurements of the fabric on hand.

If you don't want to piece large backings, there is a wide range of extra-wide cotton backings made for quilts. At about 109 inches, these fabrics will cover almost any quilt in one piece. Make sure you have at least 2 inches extra all around when you trim your backing. When asking or searching for these fabrics, ask for "extra-wide quilt backing," and you should be able to find many to choose from.

Question 166:
Should I only use cotton for my backing?

Just as with your patchwork blocks, you are not limited to using only woven cotton for your backing, especially with all of the wonderful fabrics available to make your quilt warmer and cozier.

If you're making the quilt for cold-climate snuggling or for a baby, consider cotton flannel for the back. Many quilt shops carry beautiful printed flannels that can be used in the top or the backing, but you must always prewash flannels because they have a very high rate of shrinkage.

One of the nice things about using cotton flannel with a cotton needle-punched batting is that over time and with much washing, the flannel and the batting almost seem to bond together, creating a very thick, dense, and yet soft, backing for the quilt.

Microfleece (Minkee is one popular brand) is also wonderful for the backs of quilts, but it's more difficult

to work with. The super-soft, thick fleece begs for long cuddles on cold nights.

Children love microfleece backings on their quilts because it's so inviting to touch, but microfleece can be a pain to work with. The nature of microfleece makes it very squishy, for want of a better word. It moves and slides like water on a mirror. Use spray baste to join your microfleece to your batting or top. (Some fleeces are so thick, you can opt not to use batting.) You'll need to smooth the layers out carefully. Then, once your sandwich is done, iron it well from the top only (so you don't ruin the fleece's nap) to smooth out any hidden puckers. Then you're ready to quilt.

Lightweight wools, silks, and velvets can be used as backs as well, but are not as common. You'll need to experiment with these fabrics to find out how they hold up to quilting and washing.

Question 167:
What is batting and what kind should I use?

"Batting" is the middle layer of a quilt and usually provides some loft or dimension for the quilting.

The type of batting used is a personal decision, based on the project's needs and the quilter's preferences.

Battings are made from an assortment of materials, including cotton, polyester, wool, silk, bamboo, and, most recently, recycled soda bottles (I kid you not!). Some wool and cotton battings require prewashing, but there are plenty of brands available that don't.

The choice of batting to use is mostly determined by the type of quilting you'll be doing. Different techniques, including hand-quilting, machine-quilting, and tying the quilt, have different batting requirements. A batting that works great for hand-quilting might not be the best choice for machine-quilting.

What will be the quilt's final use? If the quilt will be hung, you probably don't want a very fluffy batting. If your quilt will be snuggled under, a fluffier batting might make more sense. Wool battings can make the quilt warmer. Polyester batting can also be warm to lie under. All-cotton battings tend to be breathable and might be good for warmer climates.

How dense will your quilting be? Some battings recommend quilting every two inches, others can have the quilting spaced as far apart as ten inches. This makes a big difference to the quilting design. Most battings will have the recommended spacing for quilting printed on the wrapper.

If, as a beginner, you're looking for a good all-around batting to get you started, I recommend all-cotton, needle-punched battings, especially the kind that don't require prewashing. Cotton battings look flatter and more traditional than other choices.

Whatever batting you try, first make a test by layering the batting between fabrics and quilting it in the technique you prefer. Write the name of the batting on the test piece. This personal reference library of batting will help you as you progress with your quilting skills. You can refer back to it in the future.

Question 168:

What is a quilt sandwich, and how do I make one?

A quilt 'sandwich' is made from a quilt top, a batting layer in the middle, and a backing. Most quilters cut the batting and backing at least 2 inches larger all around the edges of the top to allow for any 'shrinkage' that happens during the quilting. If your top measures 50 inches by 70 inches, your batting/backing layers need to be at least 54 inches by 74 inches. You'll trim the excess when you've finished quilting.

Follow the guidelines above to calculate the yardage and piecing. Make sure every layer of your sandwich is ironed as smoothly as possible. You don't want any puckers or crinkles. Make your sandwich by placing the backing right-side down on a large surface. For smaller quilts, work on a dining table or counter, but large quilts need more room. Many local quilt shops allow quilters to use their classroom space to sandwich quilts.

Next, place the batting on top. Most batting comes large enough to cover the backing. The exception could be a king-sized quilt, where you might need to stitch together pieces of batting to meet the width.

The stitching is done by hand with a simple X stitch on the overlap, which is then trimmed down as closely as possible to the stitching to avoid creating too much bulk at the seam. Spread the batting from the center outward on the backing. It's important that the batting is as smooth as possible.

The quilt top comes next. If your top is big, you may need an extra pair of hands to help you open up the quilt top and place it correctly on top of the batting. Again, make sure it's well pressed, and that the seams are lying flat and in the correct direction. If your seams are poorly pressed or if they are flip-flopped along their length, they will create added bulk for your quilting, which, in turn, could distort the quilt.

Spread the top on the batting, smoothing out from the center to the edges, and you're ready to baste in a traditional manner (using thread or pins as follows). If you're spray basting, you'll handle this a little differently. "Basting" is temporarily joining the layers together so that you can quilt the sandwich.

Question 169:
How do I baste a quilt?

Once your sandwich is complete, you're ready to baste your quilt. The oldest, most traditional way to baste your quilt is with needle and thread. Any type or color of thread can be used, since it won't be staying in your quilt.

Place your quilt sandwich, top-side up, on a firm surface. Use the longest needle you have and starting from one corner, stitch long stitches (at least 8 inches) diagonally until you reach the opposite corner. The firm surface will offer leverage for your needle. Repeat between the other corners. Then stitch a cross through the quilt, north to south and east to west. If your quilt is really big, you'll probably need to do more stitching.

The goal is to crisscross the quilt until there are no very large areas that are not secured. After you've quilted your quilt, you will pull the long basting threads out.

For pin basting, again place your sandwich on a firm surface. You'll need enough large safety pins to place a pin about every 2 to 3 inches all over the quilt. Pinning can be very hard on your fingers, but there are tools on the market to help you close the pins.

After your quilt is pin-basted, you can quilt as desired, but you must remove the pins before you stitch over them. This takes time, but it's a trusted alternative to thread basting.

Question 170:
What is spray basting and is it better?

Spray basting is a much quicker alternative to pin or thread basting, and it's the only method I use, regardless of the size or type of quilt I'm basting. Spray baste is a temporary spray can adhesive made for fabric. I always use 505 Spray and Fix®. It's acid-free, washes out of the fabric and won't gum up your sewing machine needle. There are other brands on the market, but I'm loyal to 505—I've never had a problem with it, and the smell of some of the other sprays is too harsh for me.

The reasons I prefer spray baste are: It takes only minutes to baste even a king-size quilt; the adhesive lasts forever—you can to reactivate it with a steam iron; it's repositionable, so if your sandwich has a pucker in it, you can lift and resmooth the fabric; you can let your quilt sit for years without worrying about the spray baste wearing off (yes, I've tested this); and it provides the best possible surface for machine quilting because every part of the sandwich is evenly adhered through all the layers.

The instructions for spray basting provided here differ slightly from the manufacturer's recommendations, but it's worked for me for years.

Work in a well-ventilated room or in the open air, as long as there is no wind or fan-driven air movement to move the spray around. You don't want to blow the spray chemicals into your face! If you're sensitive to the spray baste's smell, use a face mask.

Place the backing, wrong-side up, on a firm surface. Make sure the backing is smooth. Place the batting on top of the backing. When they are both smoothed out, peel the batting halfway back onto itself. This exposes half of the backing's wrong side and half of the batting's side. Hold the can about 12 inches above the fabric and with a light touch,

spray the entire exposed surfaces of both the backing and the batting. Do this quickly and evenly making sure there is an extra moment of spraying for the corners. Then, carefully and slowly, smooth the batting onto the wrong side of the backing. Work with your hand flat, smoothing from the center to the edges. When done, repeat with the other half of the backing.

Once the backing and batting are bonded, carefully lay the top, wrong-side down, onto the batting. Again, make sure the seams are well-ironed in place. You might need an extra pair of hands. The batting/ backing combo still needs to be at least 2 inches larger all around than the top.

Once the top is in place, fold it back onto itself halfway. Spray evenly and quickly, covering the exposed batting and the top's wrong side. Then, as before, smooth the top back onto the batting, from the center out to the edges. Repeat with the other half of the top.

When done, iron the sandwich from the center outward with a hot, steam iron. This "sets" the fabric and makes the adhesive adhere better. At this point you can take as much or as little time as you want to quilt your project. If the sandwich seems to split apart at some point in the future, just steam iron again to reactivate the adhesive.

Some quilters believe that spray baste gums up their sewing machine needles. Yes, there is eventually a little gumming of the needles, but by then you should have changed the needle anyway. For me, the time- and labor-saving benefits of spray-basting far outweigh tossing the needles.

Question 171:

What's the best way to make sure my finished quilt hangs flat?

If ever there was one factor in a quilt that separates the amateur from the pro, it's how the quilt hangs when it's displayed.

A quilt with wavy edges looks unprofessional, but it can be hard to achieve a quilt that's completely flat. A flat quilt comes from a combination of accurate piecing, even and balanced quilting, smooth sandwiching, good trimming, and perfect binding. When you've achieved all of this, and added a sleeve correctly, your quilt should hang straight and proud. If it's slightly wavy, you can try to iron your quilt well with a hot steam iron. This acts as a blocking method of sorts and can amend some of the problems. Unless it is an art quilt that should never meet water, wash it first and then iron.

Storing your quilt will also affect its ability to hang straight. Deep fold lines will distort your quilt. Many quilt owners store their quilts on extra beds (layered one on top of another), on a rack where they can be spread out, rolled on long tubes, or folded but refolded frequently to offset creasing. Quilts stored on shelves should be rotated regularly to allow for air circulation.

Question 172:
What's the point of machine-quilting my quilt?

Machine-quilting gives a quilt a different texture from hand-quilting. Depending on the preference and skill of the quilter, a quilt can have an open, all-over design, or be "custom" quilted with different motifs in different areas of the quilt.

Machine-quilting can be achieved using many home sewing machines. For straight designs, the machine's feed dogs are left up or raised and the feed dogs help move the quilt sandwich under the presser foot and needle. Even-feed or "walking" feet are also used to help all three layers of the quilt sandwich to move evenly under the foot and needle, preventing puckers and tucks in the fabric.

Free-motion machine-quilting is usually achieved by dropping or covering the feed dogs on the sewing machine, which allows the quilt sandwich to flow unhindered in any direction under the foot and needle. Using free-motion quilting, almost any design can be accomplished. It's like doodling or drawing with the needle and thread, and the quilting effects can be

ABOVE Machine-quilting.

gorgeous. But free-motion quilting takes patience and practice to master.

At its most basic, machine-quilting is a huge timesaver compared with hand-quilting, though the more detailed the design work, the more time it will take to complete a quilt. It wasn't too long ago that quilters turned their noses up at machine-quilting, considering it an inferior form of finishing for any quilt. But, in the last thirty years machine-quilting has come into its own, and today, with the advent of professional longarm and mid-arm quilters ready to do the job for a fee, it's a perfectly acceptable way to finish a quilt.

Question 173:
What is longarm quilting?

Longarm quilting is a specific type of machine-quilting produced on a different kind of sewing machine (called a longarm) and a huge frame system, sometimes with a computer interface. A longarm machine has a large harp, which allows for the machine to sew deeply into the quilt. Usually it's mounted on a frame and the operator guides the machine from above, moving the machine's needle over the quilt with a grip system. The quilt is rolled onto a large frame which usually allows the quilt's entire width to be pulled taut. The quilt's length is rolled along the rollers, and the operator periodically unrolls a fresh section of the quilt and rolls up the section just completed.

Modern longarm systems offer computer interfaces which provide pre-programmed quilting patterns. Many longarm quilters hire out their services to quilters wanting someone else to finish a quilt for them, and pre-programmed quilting patterns can save time. The average fee for quilting a queen-sized bed quilt with a simple, overall pattern is $135, according to the American Professional Quilting Systems Web site in 2010 (www.APQS.com). Custom work demands more skill and time, and prices are higher accordingly. Fees also vary from region to region.

Longarm machines are capable of incredibly beautiful custom work and all major quilt shows now acknowledge the skills presented by longarmers, with special classes and awards just for machine quilting.

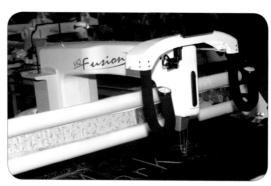

RIGHT Longarm quilting machine.

Question 174:
How do I prepare to machine-quilt my quilt?

Machine-quilting takes practice and patience to master, but there are several ways to make the job easier. The tips I'm offering here are the methods and tools that have worked best for me over the years. These tips will give you a starting point for machine-quilting. Machine-quilting can be done in many different ways to achieve the same result. Your job is to figure out what works best for you.

Start by putting together your quilt sandwich following the suggestions for spray basting, and pressing your sandwich before you start quilting, as described on page 187.

If you're working on your home sewing machine, clear the area around the machine. If your machine is flush-mounted into a tabletop or sewing desk, that's great. If it's not and you have an optional table for your machine that will provide a level surface around the machine's bed, use it. The bigger the area flush to your machine's needle, the better you'll be able to manipulate the quilt's bulk as you sew.

If you're working on a large quilt, twin-sized, or bigger, try bringing an ironing board close to your sewing area to help support the bulk of the quilt. Lower the board until it's the same height as the table or desk top.

Finally, good lighting will be your best friend while you're machine-quilting, especially for free-motion work. You have to be able to see where you're moving the quilt while it's being stitched. If you have a daylight lamp, position it so that the light shines directly on the sewing machine's bed. There are several manufacturers who make daylight lamps for hobbyists, from small, folding portable models to large floor lamps with added features like magnifying glasses and shelves.

Question 175:
Are special materials needed for machine-quilting?

Here is a list of the basics needed for successful machine-quilting. Remember, there might be several variations of these tools, and something not listed here might work better for you. Ultimately, always use what you like best.

- New sewing machine needles—at least five;
- Top thread for your quilt;
- Bobbin thread for your quilt (may or may not be the same as the top thread);
- Marking tools if you're marking designs on the quilt's top;
- Quilter's glove or traction paddles for moving the quilt under the needle;
- Darning or free-motion foot for your sewing machine;
- Walking or even-feed foot for your sewing machine (if your machine has one available—some older models and lower cost models may not have the option);
- Single needle plate for your sewing machine, if available;
- Extension table if your sewing machine doesn't sit flush in your sewing table;
- Empty bobbins;
- Additional task lighting.

When you're first starting out with machine-quilting, don't go crazy and buy everything on this list. Try the technique and decide whether you really want to do this. You will need thread, needles, darning foot, something for traction, and marking tools if you're marking designs, but you probably already have these. In time, you can add the other items on the list. You'll likely find that each provides just a little more help with your machine-quilting.

Question 176:
What kind of thread do I use for the top stitching?

Quilters' opinions vary about what thread to use. Some believe that using only cotton in your top and bobbin threads is best, as the cotton thread is the same weight and strength as the fabric and will wear at the same rate as the quilt. These quilters assert that using synthetic threads, which are stronger than cotton, will cause the quilting stitches to tear through the cotton fabric over time.

Other quilters don't worry too much about this and use whatever threads suit their design.

The kind of thread you use can make a great difference in your quilting, both with how it flows through the needle and how it ultimately looks on the quilt. These days you can use whatever thread you like as long as you know which needle and tension handles the thread best. The exception would be very thick or heavy threads that are specifically marked as being for "bobbin work." These threads provide a special effect and can only be used in the bobbin.

For your first time, use a high-quality cotton thread that will

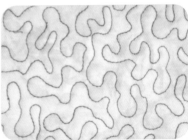

ABOVE Examples of different machine quilting with the same variegated thread.

blend into the quilt's background colors. As you improve, you'll want to showcase your quilting more and then you can use contrasting thread colors. Look for 40 to 60 weight, long-staple cotton threads. You'll want to buy at least two spools for a bed-sized quilt. Variegated threads, with color changes every inch or so in the thread, offer added dimension to the quilting and are fun to use.

Question 177:
Should I use the same thread in the bobbin as on top?

In my experience, the threads used on top are not always the easiest to use in the bobbin. Top threads are attractive when they are thicker, and bobbins seem to perform better with a thinner thread.

My favorite threads for machine quilting are Bottom Line by Libby Lehman (made by Superior Threads) and Aurifil's line of 60-weight cotton threads.

Libby is a well-known machine-quilter who "paints" with thread. Her Bottom Line thread is a 60 weight, long-staple polyester thread that moves through the bobbin casing like a hand through air. Because it's synthetic, there's very little lint. Best of all, because the thread is so thin,

you can wind more onto a bobbin, which means fewer bobbin changes.

Aurifil's performance is similar to Bottom Line because it's also thin and long-staple, but it is made from cotton and many quilters like the purity of using only cotton in their quilting.

For the bobbin thread either select a color that blends into the quilt's backing, or one which matches the top thread's color, which will help camouflage any tension problems with the stitching.

If you can't find these brands, try an alternative good-quality cotton thread, the thinner, the better. If there's a problem, your machine will tell you pretty quickly.

Question 178:
What needles should I use?

The choice of needle depends on the weight and thickness of the thread and what it's made from.

Most cotton threads work fine with sharp, quilting or universal needles.

For any other type of specialty threads, such as rayon, polyester or silk, a topstitch needle might work better. A topstitch needle has a longer groove in the back through which the thread travels. This groove results in less pulling and snagging on the thread, which means fewer thread breaks.

Never skimp on your machine needles! Working with a dull needle will cause you far more stress than replacing it. Dull needles lead to skipped stitches, broken thread, and bad tension. A rough guess as to how many needle changes you can expect while you're machine-quilting is about one needle for every two bobbins.

Question 179:
Can I use invisible thread?

If you don't want your quilting to show on the top of the quilt, invisible thread can be a good option, and it can also be used in the bobbin. But be warned that invisible thread can be very tricky, and you need to know some rules to quilt with it successfully.

First, use the correct machine needle. I use a topstitch needle, either 80/12 or 90/14 size. Because the topstitch needle's groove provides less friction as the thread moves through the needle, there is less snagging and breaking of your thread. Topstitch needles can be hard to track down. Look for online sources or ask your local shop to order them in bulk for you.

When quilting with invisible thread, slow down your quilting speed a little. Invisible threads are made from synthetics, and as they move through the fabric, the threads heat and stretch. If you slow down your stitching speed, the thread will stretch less.

Also, you'll probably need to lower your thread tension, which will require some testing on your practice quilt sandwich. Make only very slight adjustments to the tension knob and try it out each time. When the tension looks correct, write down what the settings are along with what kind of thread is in the bobbin.

Finally, when winding your bobbin with invisible thread, here are two tips. Gently place your finger on the top of the spinning bobbin to slow the winding process down so that there is less heat and less stretch. And only wind the bobbin halfway. You will have to rewind the bobbin more often, but there will be less stretching of the thread.

Question 180:
What is stippling?

In machine-quilting, an all-over stitching pattern that randomly repeats and meanders across the quilt is called "stippling." Most quilters think that stippling is only that pattern which curves and curls, like a jigsaw puzzle, but in fact it refers to the overall nature of the pattern. Stippling can look like hearts, loops, zigzags, circles, or wiggles, and feels almost like scribbling. Its purpose is to fill spaces attractively. Stippling can be done in big, open patterns or small, tight designs, depending on the quilt's needs.

Every decent machine-quilter should have at least one or two stippling designs in his or her design library because this is the quickest way to get that quilt quilted.

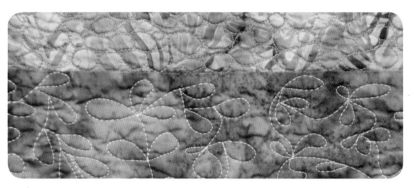

Question 181:
What about feathers, ropes, and medallion patterns?

Feathers are another standard quilting pattern, and can be created freehand (without stencils) or sewn over stenciled or drawn patterns. Stenciled feathers suggest a traditional quilt and can be quite formal. Freehand feathers are lighter, varying in size and shape, and suit a more contemporary quilt.

Similar to feathers, ropes are also a traditional design and are often found in a quilt's borders. Two or more "twisted" lengths of stitching look like rope when done correctly. Not many quilters try freehand ropes; they just don't seem to come out right. But there are plenty of stencils of rope patterns available to mark your quilt and enable you to stitch accurately.

Medallion patterns are used mostly in featured open spaces on the quilt, such as when alternate blocks of solid fabrics are used between patchwork blocks. Corners are also good areas for medallion quilting. Again, as with feathers and ropes, medallions lean more to the traditional end of quilting.

Question 182:
What about stencils and other set quilt patterns?

Since machine-quilting is so popular, there are literally thousands of quilting stencils available with which to mark your quilt and guide your quilt stitching. Usually made from heavy-duty but flexible plastic, these stencils can be used over and over. Stencils are available at local quilt shops and fabric stores, as well as online and in catalogs. You can also make your own quilting stencils by purchasing stencil plastic from a craft store and "carving" your pattern with a craft knife.

Another option for quilting is a continuous-line quilt pattern. Often found in books but sometimes sold as separate packages, continuous-line quilt patterns are printed on lightweight paper that can sometimes be pinned to the quilt top and sewn through, or can be traced onto template plastic and then cut for use. These patterns are especially helpful for machine-quilting because they are designed to minimize the number of times you'll need to stop and start your stitching.

Question 183:
How do I mark quilting patterns on my quilt top?

Patterns can be marked on the quilt top using special washable or erasable fabric pens or markers; with transfer paper; from stencils using chalk or markers; or by paper patterns that are sewn through.

When using any of the fabric markers made for quilt tops, make sure to test first on a scrap of fabric. Read the instructions very carefully. Many markers can be set by the heat of an iron; some are removed by the iron. Some like water; others do not. A popular transfer medium is chalk. Chalk will erase or wash out of most fabrics. There are even methods for marking using loose chalk powder. One manufacturer has powdered chalk in an aerated bag. You "pounce" the chalk bag over the stencil and the chalk passes through the open spaces of the stencil's design to mark the quilt top underneath. Chalk comes in different colors: white is the obvious choice for dark fabrics; pink or blue is better for white fabric. Make sure you can see the lines and that the chalk can be removed from your fabric test piece.

Question 184:
So how do I free-motion quilt?

Thread the machine, wind the extra bobbins, and install the free-motion or darning foot. If you have one, install your single-needle plate and change to a fresh needle.

Look at your quilt and make a loose plan. Doodle some quilt patterns and look in quilting books and magazines for ideas.

When you're ready, make sure your needle is in the "up" position and lift the presser foot. Slide the quilt sandwich under the foot until you get to the quilt's center. Just as in hand-quilting, you want to stitch from the center outward in order to prevent puckers. Work on small sections at a time, and make sure you have good light to work by.

In machine-quilting, the section of your quilt being stitched needs to be held taut so that no puckers or folds are created. Spread your hands flat on the quilt top to even the fabric's tension around the machine needle. Use your hands to maneuver the quilt as you stitch.

Free-motion machine-quilting requires patience and practice. You need to get used to working with a faster speed and you have to practice keeping your stitch length consistent. Over time, this will become easier.

It will help if the area is well-lit and if your quilt is at the appropriate height for sewing. If your machine is not set into a table top, creating a flush work surface, you might find it awkward. If you can, use an extension table to level the quilting area. You might also need to raise the height of your chair and possibly work with a foot stool to compensate for the new height. It's very important not to work with your shoulders at an unnatural angle.

At the start of any machine-quilting session, work on a practice piece to loosen up your shoulders and hands. When you're ready to work on your project, commit to stopping every 20 to 30 minutes to stretch. It's easy to cause repetitive motion problems by quilting, and frequent breaks will help prevent this.

Question 185:
How do I perfect my machine quilting?

When I first learned to machine-quilt, it seemed that nothing worked very well, and I struggled with thread tension. So I did what all diligent quilters do: I whined to my experienced quilting friends and gathered their advice! Armed with their suggestions, I put together a list of materials and tools that helped me to conquer free-motion machine-quilting.

Every sewing machine has its own personality—what it does and doesn't like and what adjustments work best. My machine did not like standard thread in the bobbin. When I switched to thin, high-quality threads (50 and 60 weight), my stitch tension immediately improved and I had less thread breakage. The single-needle plate also made a huge difference. With it, my needle didn't "punch" the fabric through the machine's base into the bobbin casing and workings, as it did with the zigzag plate which many machines have installed as the default plate. Lastly, having traction of some kind was essential for moving my quilt sandwich freely under the needle. The technique is called "free-motion" because you are moving the quilt under the needle at your own speed and in any direction, forward, backward, or sideways. But if your hands are slipping on the quilt, that movement will be impeded. The last tip was to lower my top thread's tension slightly, from 4 to 3.5 on my machine. This put an end to pulled stitches.

Write down every successful change you make to your machine-quilting. This becomes your record of what works best for your machine and technique.

Question 186:
How do I pull my threads out of sight on the back of the quilt?

When you start to sew, lower your needle into the quilt by hand (turning the wheel) and then raise it up. As you raise the needle, the top thread will be looped with the bobbin thread. Make sure your foot is off the machine's pedal so you don't accidentally stitch your fingers! Pull the top thread's tail, and you'll see the bobbin thread's loop come up through the hole you just made. Put small scissors or a stiletto into the loop and pull the bobbin thread up until you find the tail. Then, holding both the top thread's and the bobbin thread's tails to the side of the needle, take a couple of stitches where they came up. This will secure the threads to the quilt. Snip the threads close to the stitches and start quilting.

When you've finished quilting, you can repeat this process or you can leave your thread tails in the quilt's back. If you leave the threads on the back, tie the two threads together to make a secure knot and then use a small needle to draw the tails back into the quilt's middle layer (batting). Master quilters never leave thread tails showing on their quilts, front or back.

187 What is binding?

188 How do I prep my quilt's edges for the binding?

189 Does it matter how wide the binding is?

190 I'm bound and determined to make a binding. What do I do?

191 Oh no! Corner ahead. What do I do?

192 What's the best way to join the binding?

193 How do I knot my thread ends?

194 How do I stitch down the binding?

195 What are quilt labels?

196 How do I attach the label to the quilt?

197 What is a sleeve, and how do I make one?

198 How do I wash my quilt?

199 Why should I keep a quilt journal?

200 What makes a great quilt?

14

BINDING AND FINISHING

Question 187:
What is binding?

Bindings are strips of fabric wrapped around the quilt's raw edges that protect and finish the quilt. Usually, a quilt's edges will receive the most damage, so it's important for the quilt's durability to master binding.

There are several different types of binding: single-fold bindings, double-fold bindings, and edge-turned bindings. There are also decorative variations on bindings, such as prairie points, cordings, and facings.

A single-fold binding is one layer of a fabric strip that has a ¼-inch seam allowance folded over to the binding's wrong side. When the binding is attached to the quilt, there will be only one layer of fabric to cover the edges.

A double-fold binding uses a strip of fabric folded in half lengthwise, which is sewn to the quilt's front along the raw edge and folded to the back before tacking it down.

In my opinion, most quilts wear best with a double-fold binding. Double-folds are more durable and give greater protection to the quilt's edges. It's easy to master and simpler to achieve than a single-fold binding. The instructions that follow are for working with a double-fold binding.

Question 188:
How do I prep my quilt's edges for the binding?

This is another area where I tend to do things differently from the norm, but I have had consistent success. When the quilt has been completely quilted, I iron it as flat as possible. If I'm working on an embellished quilt I might go easy ironing the sections with the embellishments, but I want to have a really flat quilt top. Then, I spread the quilt over a large cutting mat, covering a dining table or other large surface, and trim the quilt's edges, as follows:

Take a 15-inch square ruler and a 8 ½ by 24-inch ruler. (Ruler sizes close to these also work.) Beginning at one long edge and working from the bottom up, place the square ruler in one corner of the quilt and use the 45-degree mark to line up the ruler evenly against the corner. Trim all three quilt layers to make the crispest line possible. While the square ruler is in position, use the longer ruler to establish the first cutting line along the quilt's long edge. I try to make an even cut parallel to the first straight seam line I can refer to—usually in the border. If the border is about 6 ½ inches, trim it to 6 ¼ inches using the border seam line as your guide. Make sure your quilt is as flat and straight as possible for this first cut because it will be used to square up the remaining cuts. With the rulers in place (double and triple check to make sure they are where they need to be—you can't reverse a bad cut!), cut along the rulers' edges from the

bottom up with a rotary cutter. If the edges are longer than the rulers, cut three-quarters of the way along the ruler and then slide it up, making sure the bottom half of the ruler edge continues to follow exactly the cut you just made. When you get close to the next corner, use the square ruler to square it off, turn the quilt so that the next edge is facing you correctly, and continue with the combination of long-ruler and square-ruler cuts.

In this way, you should end up with the straightest possible quilt edges. If the quilt is folded in half, your corners and edges should meet up perfectly.

Question 189:
Does it matter how wide the binding is?

This is another matter of the quilter's preference and I've noticed that British and Australian quilters tend to like a wider binding as well, whereas American quilters like the binding to be narrower. I prefer to use double-fold bindings on my quilts because they stand up to wear better and I find them easier to make. I also like to have a wider strip of binding showing on the back of my quilt.

If you're working with a 2 ½-inch strip that's folded in half to create a 1 ¼-inch doubled strip, and you sew it down with a ¼ inch seam allowance, you'll have ½ inch of binding to tack down to the quilt's back. Some quilters prefer a narrower binding on the back, I find it's easier to maneuver a wider binding.

Question 190:
I'm bound and determined to make a binding. What do I do?

First determine how much fabric is needed for the binding. To make a double-fold binding, calculate how many strips of binding fabric you'll need to cut by adding the measurements in inches of your quilt's four sides. A 90-inch square quilt will need 360 inches of binding. Add an additional 20 inches to that number for overage, mitered corners, and joining the strips. So you'll need at least 380 inches of binding. Working with the 40-inch width of the fabric, divide 380 by 40 to determine how many strips you'll need to cut. The answer is 9.5, so round that up to 10 strips. Then, multiply 10 by how wide your strips will be. In this case, it's 2 ½ inches, which means you'll need 25 inches of fabric cut into (10) 2½-inch strips.

Fold your fabric in half lengthwise and cut your strips from fold to selvage, making sure you're cutting accurately with your rotary ruler. To sew the strips together, take two strips, right sides together, and position them at right angles to each other. The front strip will slightly overlap the back strip. Draw a pencil line along the diagonal, pin, and then sew along that line. Trim the seam to ¼ inch with scissors. Open and press the seam to reduce bulk. Repeat with the next strip and so on until they are all joined together.

When your strips are joined, starting from one end, fold the strip in half lengthwise and press. Make the raw edges meet accurately. I then keep the binding wound on a piece of cardboard until it's time to use it, which prevents it from wrinkling.

Question 191:
Oh no! Corner ahead. What do I do?

The way you cover corners correctly in binding is called mitering. Pin the binding to the front of the quilt, exactly matching the open edge of the folded binding to the quilt's trimmed edge. Leaving an 8-inch tail, sew the binding to the quilt's edge with a ¼-inch seam allowance. Make sure not to sew over the pins but to remove them as you go along. Stop stitching about a ¼ inch from the corner. Backstitch to secure, clip the threads, and remove the quilt from the sewing machine.

Place the quilt edge you've just sewn on the ironing board front side up. Take the binding and fold it up and away from the quilt's edge at a 45-degree angle (Fig.1). Then fold the binding back down over itself and onto the next edge of the quilt (Fig.2). Press quickly into place and pin the corner. Turn the quilt so that you're working on the next edge, pin the binding in place along the edge, and start sewing again from the corner, back-stitching first, with a ¼-inch seam allowance (Fig. 3). Repeat this for the other three corners. Then fold binding to the back of the quilt and stitch in place (Fig. 4).

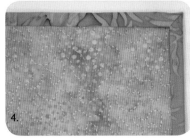

Question 192:
What's the best way to join the binding?

This can be a little tricky, but practice will make perfect. You've sewn most of the binding to the quilt's front, and you've left tails at both ends. When you reach the tail at the binding's start, stop sewing. Unfold the binding, take the two ends and overlap them until they are in line with the quilt's edge. Sew a seam to join the two ends, trim the seam to ¼ inch, press open the seam and refold the binding. Pin in place and finish sewing. The binding is now completely attached to the quilt.

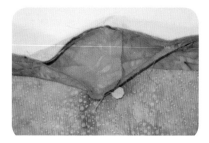

ABOVE Joining binding.

Question 193:
How do I knot my thread ends?

Start your piecing by knotting your thread with a quilter's knot. Thread your needle and make one tail longer than the other. Hold your needle in your sewing hand parallel to the floor or table, with the needle's point facing the opposite hand. Take the longer tail in your free hand and overlap it around the needle. It will look like a big loop. Hold the thread and the needle securely in your sewing hand and tightly wrap the thread over the needle four times with your other hand. With your sewing hand holding the loops in place, slowly pull the needle and thread through the loops with your non-sewing hand until you reach the bottom of the longer tail. You should have a perfect knot sitting near the bottom of the thread. Trim the end ¼ inch below the knot and you're ready to go. This will take a little practice to perfect, but it's worth it.

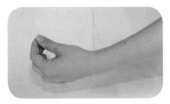

1. Take longer tail and overlap around needle.

2. Hold wraps in place.

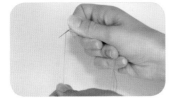

3. Tightly wrap thread around needle four times.

4. Gently pull needle through wraps.

Question 194:

How do I stitch down the binding?

A slip stitch, also called a blind stitch is the best method for tacking the binding down to the quilt's back. A slip stitch can be almost invisible from the front.

Hold the quilt on your lap with the backing facing you and the bound edge closest to you. You're looking at the binding. Using a hand needle and a 20-inch length of thread with a quilter's knot in the end. Come up on your first stitch through the front of the binding. Go back into the backing layer and travel the needle just under the backing to the left (or right if you're left-handed) for about a ¼ inch, then bring the needle up

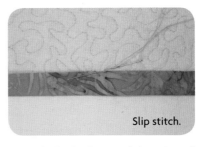

Slip stitch.

through the backing and the edge of the binding. Come back down again into the backing layer just above the edge where you came out and travel the needle through to the left again for the next stitch. Continue until you're done. At the mitered corners, take a couple of tiny stitches along the diagonal fold to hold it in place.

Question 195:
What are quilt labels?

Made from fabric and usually attached to a finished quilt's back, a quilt label is important. It identifies the quilt's owner, provides information about the quilt for future generations, offers personal thoughts for the recipient of the quilt, and gives source information about the quilt's pattern and design. What information is written on the label is up to the quilt's maker. For a quilt being shipped or being submitted to a show or contest, the label should include up-to-date contact information in case the quilt is lost.

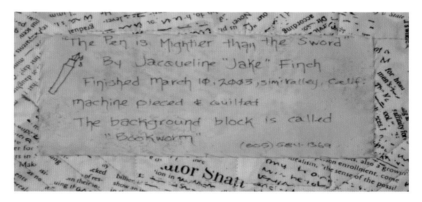

Question 196:
How do I attach the label to the quilt?

Labels can be handwritten in permanent ink with fabric pens or markers, or they can be printed onto pre-treated fabric printer sheets after being designed on a computer.

To attach a fabric label, turn under the edges to the wrong side of the label by at least a ¼ inch and press. Then slip stitch the label to the bottom corner of the back of the quilt (try to make the stitches as small and close together as possible to make it hard to cut the label off). Tie off the thread and bury the knot.

Question 197:
What is a sleeve, and how do I make one?

Quilts are often displayed hanging on walls or racks for décor, quilt shows, art exhibitions and other purposes. The best way to hang a quilt is to attach a sleeve at the top of the wrong side. A sleeve enables the quilt to be hung with an even weight distribution, which prevents quilt distortion.

Generally, a sleeve's finished size is 4 inches wide by the length of the quilt, less a few inches. This accommodates most dowels, pipes, rods or slats used in the various quilt-hanging mechanisms.

Cut a strip of fabric 5 inches wide and 6 inches less than the width of the quilt. Turn the edges ½ inch under to the wrong side along the top and bottom of the strip's length and press. Pin and then, slip stitch the sleeve's top and bottom edges along the top of the quilt's back. The top edge of the quilt sleeve should lie about 4 inches below the quilt's top finished edge, so that it's not attached to the binding. Tie off the threads ends and bury the knots.

Question 198:
How do I wash my quilt?

As a quiltmaker, if you did your job right, then a quilt can be washed without fear. In fact, over time, washing softens a quilt and makes the fibres "bond" with each other, so that its layers feel seamless.

Still, there are some common-sense methods of washing quilts in order to provide the longest life possible. First, assuming that we're not talking about antique quilts, quilts should be washed in cold water on a delicate or handwash cycle in the machine, using a mild detergent. There are detergents on the market designed specifically for quilts, but a detergent for baby clothes works fine. A harsher detergent can cause colors to fade. You can also wash a quilt by hand, in the bath if it is large.

If you're washing your quilt for the first or second time, consider throwing a dye- or color-catching sheet into the wash with the quilt and detergent to attract loose dye from fabrics.

Drying a quilt in a dryer should be fine, although the heat might shrink the fabrics slightly, especially if you didn't pre-wash them. If there is cotton, wool, silk, or a combination of these fibers in your wadding, you might find the shrinkage has scrunched up your quilt a bit. This soft, casual look is generally appreciated by quilters as it provides texture to the quilt and softens the look and feel.

Quilts with heavy embellishments that are designed to hang on the wall probably won't need to be washed, but should be dusted and vacuumed. To vacuum a quilt, spread it on a bed. Use your vacuum's hand attachment, covered with a pair of tights or some muslin, and gently run the vacuum over the quilt top. The same technique can be used to clean antique quilts.

Dry cleaning might be an option for wool or silk quilts, but only as a last-ditch alternative as the chemicals can be too harsh for delicate fibers. Try to find a cleaner who works with bridal gowns and other specialty items. You need to make sure the best care is given to your quilt, especially if it's an antique. Ensure that they will not mark the quilt in any way and will not use safety pins on the quilt.

Question 199:

Why should I keep a quilt journal?

A quilt journal is a log of the quilts you've made or that you've collected or received as gifts. It serves as a scrapbook of your work that allows you to enjoy the fruits of your labor, even if you've given your quilts away.

Beyond that, a quilt journal is a recorded history of your evolution as a quilter, and can be fun to look back on and see what styles and techniques you've enjoyed. It can be a reference for remembering where a certain pattern came from or how a project developed. And a quilt journal can become a legal reference to defend the value of a quilt should it become damaged, lost, or stolen.

A journal can be created from almost any blank book. For each entry, consider including pictures of the quilt, the quilt's name, the dimensions, when, where and why it was made, and any additional information about the design or its genesis. If the quilt has been appraised, this is a great place to keep a copy of the appraisal, as well as any receipts for materials and outsourced quilting.

Question 200:

What makes a great quilt?

When you look at a quilt and all other thought leaves your mind except for the word 'Wow', you know you're looking at a great quilt.

A great quilt is a blend of sound construction technique, excellent use of color and a harmonious design. There is balance, movement and interest. The workmanship reflects a high degree of skill. Whatever the techniques used or the style presented, a great quilt grabs the viewer's attention.

Most major quilt-show winners and popular authors spent years developing their skills and design aesthetic. So do look at quilts wearing ribbons at shows and featured in magazines and books. Study them as carefully, from the details to the overall presentation. Quilting is a visual art and much can be learned by just looking at a quilt.

Templates

Dresden Fan
Question 75, p.103.

Copy at 81%.

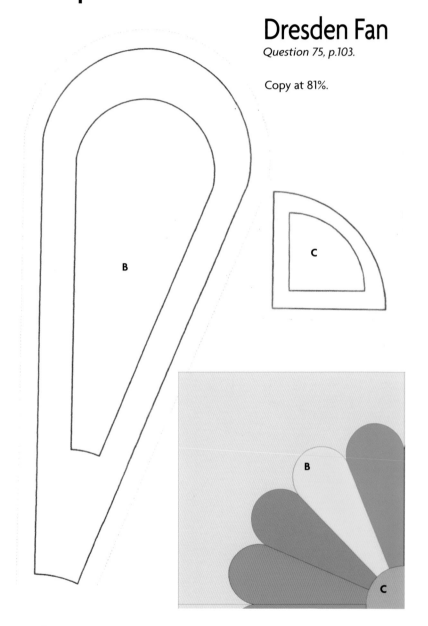

B

C

B

C

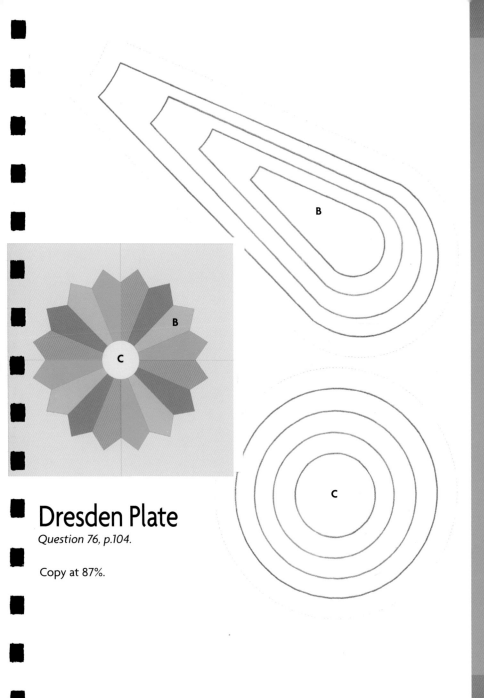

Dresden Plate

Question 76, p.104.

Copy at 87%.

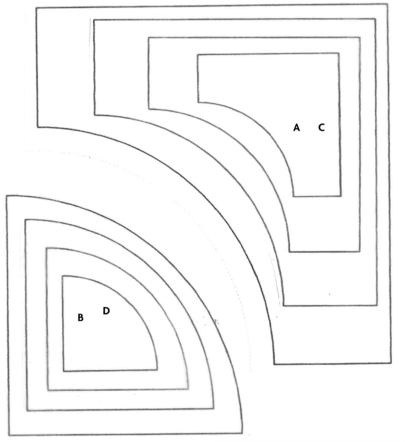

Drunkard's Path

Question 44, p.63

Enlarge by 90%.

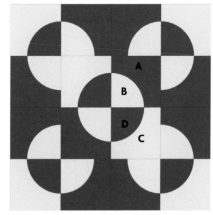

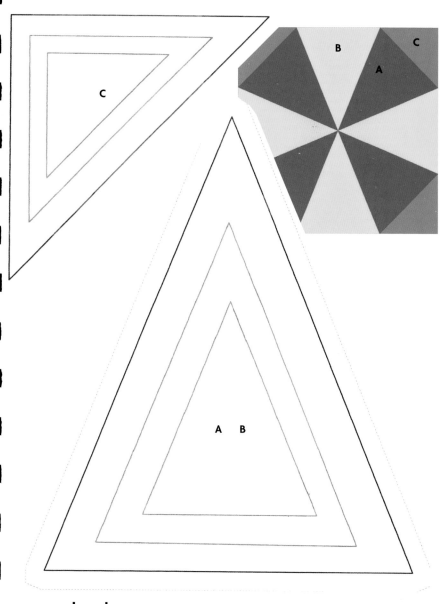

Kaleidoscope

Question 74, p.102

Enlarge by 80%.

Harlequin Star
Question 68/69, p.96/97

Enlarge by 78%.

C

To be used in the reverse as well.

House Block

Question 54, p.77

Enlarge by 55%.

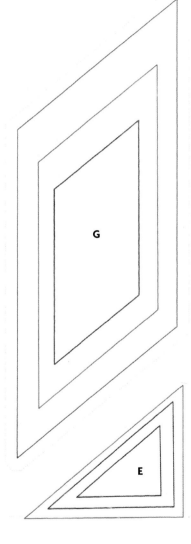

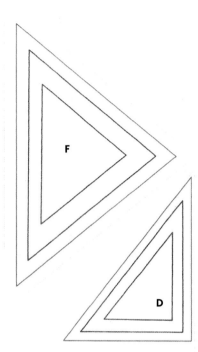

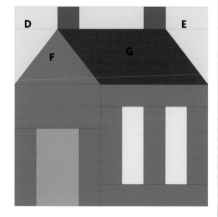

Nosegay

Question 66, p.94

Enlarge by 80%.

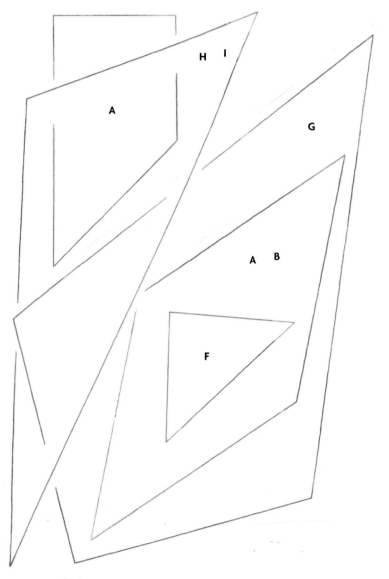

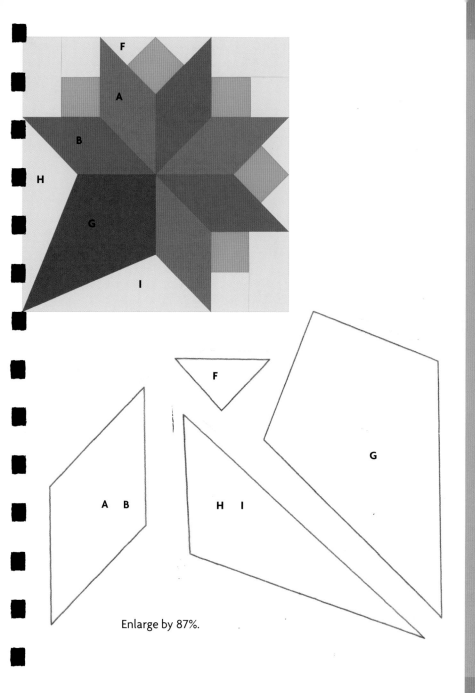

F

A

B

H

G

I

F

A B

G

H I

Enlarge by 87%.

Enlarge by 57%.

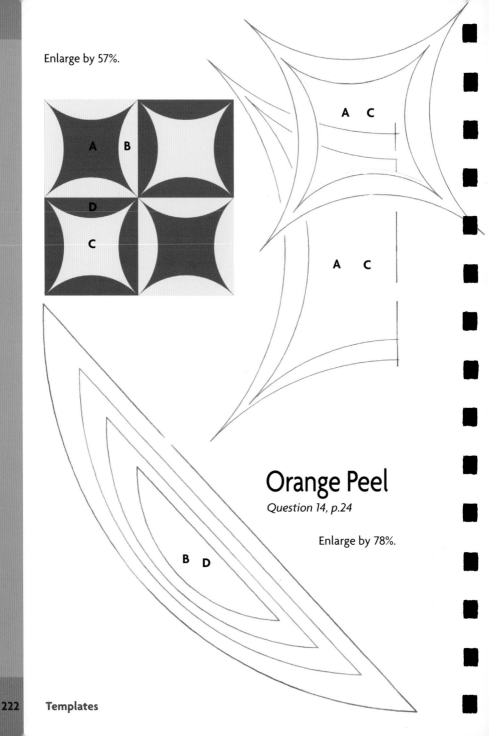

A C

A C

Orange Peel
Question 14, p.24

Enlarge by 78%.

B D

A B

D

C

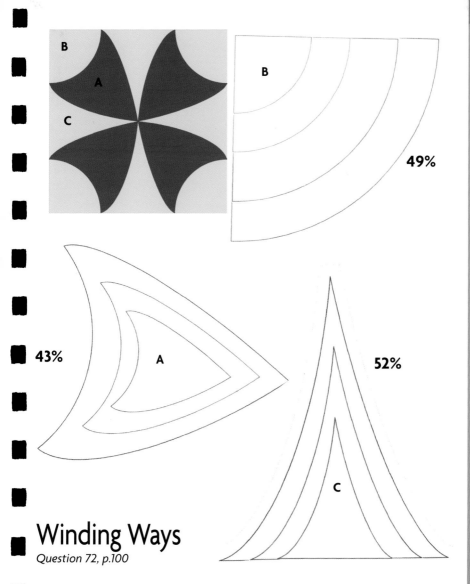

B

49%

43%

A

52%

C

Winding Ways
Question 72, p.100

Enlarge by, as above.

Index

A
appliqué, 24, 138, 171
Attic Windows blocks, 101, 167

B
backing
  fabric, 182, 184
  piecing, 183
Basket blocks, 53–54
  variations, 55–56
basting spray, 187–189
Bear Paw blocks, 31
beginners, 112
binding, 204
  corners, 207, 209
  joining, 208
  making, 206
  preparation, 204–205
  stitching down, 209
  width, 205–206
Birds in the Air blocks, 36
bleeding, 13
blocks
  choosing, 122
  design, 11
  mixing, 123
  piecing, 162–171
    borders, 177
    mitered, 178–179
    pieced, 179
    straight-cut, 178
Bow Tie blocks, 21, 165
Bridal Path blocks, 80–81
Broken Dishes blocks, 20

C
Capital T blocks, 25
Card Trick blocks, 46–47
Carpenter's Wheel blocks, 82–83
Cat's Cradle blocks, 48–49
Churn Dash blocks, 34
color
  balance, 139
  choice, 13, 126, 127
  hue, 128
  shade, 128
  tint, 129
  tone, 129
  value, 130
color schemes, 130–133
color story, 123
color wheels, 127
composition, 123
computers, 125
continuous-line quilt patterns, 198
Contrary Wife blocks, 57–58
Corner-Square triangles, 165
Courthouse Steps blocks, 87
Crossroads blocks, 98
Crown of Thorns, 59–60
curved piecing, 157
cutting mats, 114, 115

D
Delectable Mountains blocks, 79–80

design software, 125
design walls, 126
designs
  balance, 123
  block selection, 122
  color choice, 126, 127
  composition, 123
  secondary, 19
  sizes, 122
display, 189, 211
dog ears, 155
Double Nine-Patch blocks, 28–29
Double Star blocks, 95–96
Dove in the Window blocks, 40–41
Dresden Plate blocks, 104, 105
Drunkard's Path blocks, 63–64, 64
Dutch Rose blocks, 82–83
Dutchman's Puzzle blocks, 19–20

E
English patchwork, 106
EQ7, 125

F
fabric
  amounts, 124
  backing, 182, 184
  bias, 138
  choice, 136
  grain, 137–138
  pre-cut, 140–141
  preparation, 137
  quality, 113
  selection, 139
  selvage, 138
Fan blocks, 103, 105, 171
fat eighths, 141
fat quarters, 140
feathers, 197–198
Fifty-Four Forty blocks, 43
Fight blocks, 43
first quilts, 112–113
Flying Geese blocks, 17, 163
foundations, 79, 90
Four-Patch blocks, 16, 162
free-motion quilting, 199–200
Friendship Star blocks, 35
fussy cutting, 77

G
Garden Square blocks, 39–40
getting started, 112

H
Half-Square triangles, 158, 159, 164
Handy Andy blocks, 71–72
hanging, 189, 211
Harlequin Star blocks, 97
Heart blocks, 70–71
Hole in the Barn Door

blocks, 34
House blocks, 77–78
Hunter's Star blocks, 93

I
inspiration, 133
Irish Chain blocks, 58–59, 91
ironing, 115, 119

J
Jacob's Ladder blocks, 68–69
jelly rolls, 140

K
Kaleidoscope blocks, 102
King's Crown blocks, 61

L
Lady of the Lake blocks, 73
LeMoyne Star, 92
Log Cabin blocks, 86
long triangles, 168

M
machine-quilting, 190
  basic requirements, 192
  free-motion, 199–200
  longarm, 191
  needles, 195–196, 196
  patterns, 197–199
  perfecting, 200–201
  preparation, 192
  stippling, 197
  thread, 193
Maple Leaf blocks, 41–42
medallions, 198
Monkey Wrench blocks, 74

N
needles, 118–119, 148, 195–196, 196
New York Beauty blocks, 99
Nine-Patch blocks, 28
Northwinds blocks, 37–38
Nosegay blocks, 94

O
Ocean Waves blocks, 89
Ohio Star blocks, 30
Old Maid's Puzzle blocks, 23
on point setting, 176
Orange Peel blocks, 24

P
paper piecing, 158
patchwork, definition, 11
patterns, 11
  machine-quilting, 197–199
  marking, 199
  piecing, 152–153
  blocks, 162–171
  curved, 157
  paper, 158
Pine Burr blocks, 96–97, 169–170

Pine Tree blocks, 69–70
Pineapple blocks, 88
pins, 151
Pinwheel blocks, 17–18, 164
pressing, 115, 119, 154–155, 167

Q
Quarter-Square triangles, 158, 159, 166
quilt journals, 212–213
quilt labels, 210
quilting, 10
Quilt-Pro software, 125
quilts
  construction, 10, 186
  contemporary, 13
  Double Wedding Ring, 106
  first, 112–113
  Grandmother's Flower Garden, 106
  great, 214
  Lone Star, 93, 108
  Mariner's Compass, 109
  Nosegay, 94
  parts, 115
  sampler, 29, 112–113
  sizes, 122
  tacking, 187
  Thousand Pyramids, 107
  Trip Around the World, 107
  Tumbling blocks, 108
  two-blocks, 29
  washing, 211–212
  wedding, 107

R
Rail Fence blocks, 32
Road to Paradise blocks, 44–45
ropes, 198
rotary cutters, 114, 141, 143, 144
  changing blades, 142–143
rotary mats, 145
rotary rulers, 114, 145
rows
  marking, 174
  sewing, 174–175

S
sampler quilts, 29, 112–113
sashing, 175
Sawtooth Star blocks, 56, 80
seams
  accuracy, 151–152
  allowances, 124
  dog ears, 155
  nestled, 154
  pressing, 115, 154–155, 167
  Y-seams, 92, 167
secondary designs, 19
selvage, 138
sewing cabinets, 114–115
sewing machines, 113–114, 114–115. see

also machine-quilting
accessories and attachments, 117–119, 149
bobbins, 149
care, 117
choice, 116
thread tension, 150
Shadows blocks, 90
Shoofly blocks, 32–33
sketches, 123–124
skewing, 13
sleeves, 211
Snail's Trail blocks, 75–76
Snowball blocks, 62
Solomon's Puzzle blocks, 63, 64–65
Spools blocks, 22
Square in a Square format, 71, 74, 168–169
stabilizers, 79, 90
starch, 155
stencils, 198
stippling, 197
storage, 189
Storm at Sea blocks, 52–53
strip-piecing, 156

T
tacking, 187
templates, 24, 145, 214
tessellating blocks, 25
thread, 148, 150, 195–196
  invisible, 196
  machine-quilting, 193–194
  tails, 201, 208–209
tools, 113–114, 141–145
traditional patchwork, 12
triangles
  calculating size of, 159, 176
  making, 164–166, 168
Twin Star blocks, 38

Variable Star blocks, 48, 95
Virginia Reel blocks, 76

W
wadding, 185
wedding quilts, 107
Winding Ways blocks, 100
Windmill blocks, 18–19, 166
work space, 114–115

Y
Y-seams, 92, 167